Contract Law in Sweden

Contract Law in Sweden

Boel Flodgren
Eric M. Runesson

This book was originally published as a monograph in the International Encyclopaedia of Laws/Contracts.

General Editors: Roger Blanpain, Frank Hendrickx
Volume Editor: Jacques Herbots

Wolters Kluwer
Law & Business

Published by:
Kluwer Law International
PO Box 316
2400 AH Alphen aan den Rijn
The Netherlands
Website: www.kluwerlaw.com

Sold and distributed in North, Central and South America by:
Aspen Publishers, Inc.
7201 McKinney Circle
Frederick, MD 21704
United States of America
Email: customer.service@aspenpublishers.com

Sold and distributed in all other countries by:
Turpin Distribution Services Ltd.
Stratton Business Park
Pegasus Drive, Biggleswade
Bedfordshire SG18 8TQ
United Kingdom
Email: kluwerlaw@turpin-distribution.com

ISBN 978-90-411-6004-1

This title is available on www.kluwerlawonline.com

The Authors

Professor Boel Flodgren (born 1942) studied law at the University of Lund, Sweden. In 1978 she obtained her Doctorate in Law (J.S.D, LL.D.) from the same university. Her doctoral thesis was a comparative study of Swedish and US Labor Law with the title 'The Labor Union and the Law. A Comparative Study of the Right to Organize in Sweden and the United States'. She was a visiting Ph.D. student at Stanford University Law School during the academic year 1975–1976 and spent the year 1991–1992 at Harvard University Law School as a visiting researcher. For ten years (1992–2002) she was the Vice-Chancellor of Lund University. She has been awarded honorary doctorate degrees from Hanken (The Swedish School of Business Administration), Helsinki, Finland, from McGill University, Montreal, Canada and from the University of Oslo, Norway. Before and during her doctorate studies she worked as a judge in the Appeals Court in Malmö, Sweden, and as a practicing lawyer in a Swedish law firm. At present (2014) she sits on the board of two listed Swedish companies and is the chairman of a pro bono foundation. She now works as senior professor of Law at the Department of Business law, School of Economics and Management at Lund University. Boel Flodgren's research was for several years focused on Labor Law. Today, Contract Law and International Commercial Law are her primary research interests. She teaches Contract Law and International Commercial Law at the Law Faculty and at the School of Economics and Management at Lund University.

Eric M. Runesson (born 1960) studied law at Stockholm University and at Harvard Law School. He obtained his Doctorate in Law (J.S.D, LL.D.) in 1996 based on a thesis on construction of incomplete contracts. He was appointed associate professor of the Stockholm School of Economics in 2000 and served as professor adjunct at the University of Lund between 2003 and 2008. He combines his academic activities with practice as attorney. He has been partner of the lawfirm Sandart & Partners since 1993. He specialises in commercial arbitration, distribution contracts and licensing. As of 2013 he serves as board member of the Swedish Bar Association. He is author of numerous articles and books on contract law, dispute resolution and negotiation.

Table of Contents

The Authors 3

List of Abbreviations 13

Preface 15

General Introduction 17

§1. The General Background of the Country 17
I. Geography 17
II. Cultural Composition 17
III. Political History 18
IV. Political System 19
V. Economy 20
VI. Legal Culture and Legal System 21

§2. Swedish Law Belongs to the Nordic Legal Family 23

§3. Primacy of Legislation 23

§4. The Role of the Judiciary 23

§5. Between Public and Private Law ('Administrative Contracts') 24

§6. Distinction between Civil Law and Commercial Law ('Commercial Contracts') 25

Introduction to the Law of Contracts 27

§1. Definition of Contract 27
I. Will, Intent and Reliance 27
II. Freedom of Contract 28
III. Binding Character of Contract 29
IV. Mandatory Rules 30
V. Rights 'In Personam' and Rights 'In Rem' 31

§2. Historical Background of the Law of Contracts 31
I. Influence of Roman Law 31
II. Later Development of Swedish Contract Law 33

§3. Classification of Contracts 34
I. Consensual Contracts 34
II. Solemn Contracts 34
III. Real Contracts 34
IV. Bilateral and Unilateral Contracts 34
V. Onerous and Gratuitous Contracts 35
VI. Commutative and Aleatory Contracts 35
VII. Intuitu Personae Contracts 35
VIII. Nominate and Innominate Contracts 35
IX. Standard Form Contracts 36
X. Main Contracts and Accessory Contracts 36
XI. Frame Contracts 36

§4. Contract and Torts 36

§5. Contract and Quasi-contracts 38

§6. Contract and the Law of Property 39
I. No Distinction between Legal and Equitable Ownership 41
II. The Right of Usufruct 41
III. Conveyancing 42
A. Agreement 42
B. Registration 43

§7. Contract and Trust 43

§8. Good Faith and Fair Dealing 44
I. Duty of Loyalty 44
II. Duty of Cooperation 45
III. Inconsistent Behaviour 45

§9. Style of Drafting 47

§10. Sources of the Law of Contracts 47
I. The Norm Hierarchy 48
II. Practices and Custom 49

Part I. General Principles of the Law of Contract 51

Chapter 1. Formation 51

§1. Agreement and Quid Pro Quo (Reciprocity) 52

I. Offer and Acceptance 52
A. Definition of Offer 52
B. Withdrawal of Offer 54
C. Revocation of Offer 54
D. Rejection of Offer 55
E. Mode of Acceptance 55
F. Time of Acceptance 56
G. Late Acceptance 56
H. Delay in Transmission of Acceptance 57
I. Withdrawal of Acceptance 57
J. Modified Acceptance 57
K. Writings in Confirmation 58
L. Notices 59
M. Conclusion of Contracts Dependent on Agreement on Specific Matter or in a Particular Form 60
N. Contracts with a Term Deliberately Left Open 60
O. Letters of Intent 61
P. Merger Clauses and Clauses on Modification in a Particular Form 61
Q. Contracting under Standard Terms 62
R. Conflict between Standard Terms and Non-standard Terms 63
S. Battle of Forms 63
II. Intention to Create Legal Relations 64
III. Consideration 65
A. The Common Law Doctrine of Consideration 65
B. Gratuitous Promises 65

§2. Formal and Evidential Requirements 66
I. Formal Requirements 66
A. Contracts under Seal 67
B. 'Solemn' Contracts 67
II. Evidential Requirement: Proof 67
A. The Parol Evidence Rule 67
B. No Notary 67
III. Burden of Proof 67
A. General Observations on Burden of Proof 67
B. Obligation of Means and Obligation of Result 68

§3. Liability and Negotiations 69
I. Precontractual Liability 69
A. Breakdown of Negotiations 70
B. *Culpa in Contrahendo* 71
C. Duty to Inform 71
D. Intention to Contract 72
E. Damage 72
F. Summary of Precontractual Liability 72

Chapter 2. Conditions of Substantive Validity 73

§1. INVALIDITY/INTRODUCTION 73
I. General Remarks 74
II. Voidness and Voidability 75
III. Contracts Where Not All of the Terms Have Been Agreed 76
IV. The Doctrine of Impossibility 76
V. General Remarks About Formalities 76
VI. The General Clause on the Modification/Setting Aside of Contracts 77

§2. CAPACITY OF THE PARTIES 77
I. Minors 77
II. Insanity or Other Mental Disturbances 78
III. Married Women. Aliens 79
IV. Bankruptcy 79
V. Moral Person 79

§3. DEFECTS IN CONSENT 79
I. General Remarks 79
II. The Doctrine of Failed Assumptions 80
III. Duress, Coercion, Undue Influence 81
IV. Fraud 81
V. Usury (Unfair Exploitation) 82
VI. Mistake 82
A. Mistake in the Declaration of Intent 82
B. Mistake as to the Person 83
C. Mistake as to the Substance 84
VII. The General Clause on Dishonesty 84
VIII. Misrepresentation 85
IX. Gross Disparity 88

§4. OTHER CONDITIONS OF VALIDITY 88
I. Existing and Lawful Cause 88
II. Initial Impossibility 88
III. Contracts Against Public Policy 89
IV. Contracts Against Morality 89
V. Contracts Against Mandatory Regulation 90

§5. THE RE-INTEGRA RULE OF SECTION 39 OF THE CONTRACTS ACT 91

§6. THE LEGAL CONSEQUENCES OF INVALIDITY 91
I. General Remarks 91
II. Avoidance of the Contract. Nullity 91
III. Restitution 92
IV. Damages 92

Chapter 3. The Contents of a Contract 93

§1. The Different Clauses 93
I. Ascertaining of Express Terms 93
II. Implied Terms 93
III. Standard Terms and Exemption Clauses 93
IV. Penalty Clauses 93
V. Arbitration Clauses 94

§2. Interpretation 94
I. Introduction 94
II. Intention of the Parties 95
III. Interpretation of Statements and Other Conduct 95
IV. Relevant Circumstances 96
V. Reference to Contract or Statement as a Whole 98
VI. All Terms to Be Given Effect 99
VII. Contra Proferentem Rule 99
VIII. Supplying an Omitted Term 100

Chapter 4. Privity of Contract 101

§1. The Rule of Privity of Contract 101
I. Third Parties and the Contract 101
II. Contract for the Benefit of a Third Party 105
A. Conditions of Validity 106
B. The Right of the Beneficiary 106
C. Rights and Duties of the Stipulator, the Promisor and the Third Party 107
1. The Relationship Stipulator: Promisor 107
2. The Relationship Stipulator: Third Party 107
3. The Relationship Promisor: Third Party 107
D. 'Direct Actions' 107

§2. Transfer of Contractual Rights 108
I. General Principles 108
II. Effects of the Assignment 110
III. The Transfer as against Third Parties (Other Than the Debtor) 111

§3. Transfer of Contractual Obligations and of the Whole Contractual Position 111

§4. Subcontracting 112
I. The Liability of the Main Contractor for the Defective Performance of the Subcontractor 112
II. The Relationship Employer-Subcontractor 113

§5. Oblique Action, the Paulian Action and Direct Actions (Rights and Duties of Third Parties) 113

Chapter 5. The End of the Contract 115

§1. Performance 115
I. Determination of Quality of Performance 115
II. Price Determination 115
III. Contract for an Indefinite Period 116
IV. Time of Performance 116
V. Computation of Time Set by the Parties 117
VI. Partial Performance 117
VII. Order of Performance 118
VIII. Earlier Performance 118
IX. Place of Performance 118
X. Payment Methods 119
XI. Currency 119
XII. Costs of Performance 120
XIII. Imputation of Obligations 120
XIV. Application for Public Permission 120

§2. Non-performance 121
I. Non-performance Defined 121
II. Interference by the Other Party 121

§3. Impossibility, Frustration and Hardship: 'The Unforeseen' 121
I. Introduction 121
II. Modification and Cease of Obligations Due to Unforeseen Circumstances 122

§4. Discharge by Agreement 124

§5. Novation 124

Chapter 6. Remedies 125

§1. General Provisions 125

§2. Specific Performance 125

§3. Termination 126

§4. The Defence of Non-performance by the Other Party 126

§5. Damages and Exemption Clauses 127
I. Introduction 127

II. Liability for Negligence 127
III. Full Compensation 129
IV. Certainty of Harm 130
V. Foreseeability of Harm 131
VI. Proof of Harm in Case of Replacement Transaction or by Means of Current Price 132
VII. Harm Due in Part to Aggrieved Party 132
VIII. Mitigation of Harm 132
IX. Interest for Failure to Pay Money or Damages 132
X. Manner of Monetary Redress 133
XI. Currency in Which to Assess Damages 133
XII. Agreed Payment for Non-performance 134

§6. LIMITATION OF ACTIONS 134

Part II. Specific Contracts 137

Chapter 1. Agency 137

§1. REGULATION REGARDING AGENCY AND OTHER INTERMEDIARIES 137

§2. AGENCY UNDER THE CONTRACTS ACT 138
I. Various Ways to Establish Agency/Mandate 138
II. Agency as a Result of a Certain Position 139
III. The Difference between Authority and Mandate 140
IV. Termination of Agency 141
V. Ratification. Principal Becoming Bound by Passivity 141
VI. Passive Authority 141
VII. Agent Acting Outside His Authority 142

§3. COMMISSION AGENCY 142

§4. SELF-EMPLOYED COMMERCIAL AGENTS 143

§5. BROKERS 144

§6. DISTRIBUTORS 145

Chapter 2. Bailment 146

Chapter 3. Aleatory Contracts 147

§1. GAMING AND BETTING 147

Chapter 4. Sale of Goods 148

Chapter 5. Hire of Work & Skills, Building Contracts 150

§1. THE GENERAL LAW 150

§2. BUILDING CONTRACTS 153

Chapter 6. Lease, Commercial and Agricultural Leases 155

Chapter 7. Compromise Settlement 157

Chapter 8. Suretyship 158

Chapter 9. Pledge 159

Chapter 10. Loans 161

Chapter 11. Contracts with the Government and Other Public Administrations 162

Chapter 12. Contract of Partnership 164

Chapter 13. Quasi-contracts 165

§1. NEGOTIORUM GESTIO 165

§2. ENRICHMENT WITHOUT CAUSE 165

§3. MONEY PAID BUT NOT DUE (*CONDICTIO INDEBITI*) 166

Selected Bibliography 167

Index 169

List of Abbreviations

AD	Arbetsdomstolen
BGB	Bürgerliches Gesetzbuch
CISG	Convention on Contracts for the International Sale of Goods
	HFD Högsta förvaltningsdomstolen
JT	Juridisk Tidsskrift
MD	Marknadsdomstolen
NJA	Nytt Juridiskt Arkiv
RH	Rättsfall från hovrätterna
RÅ	Regeringsrättens Årsbok
UNIDROIT	International Institute for the Unification of Private Law
UPICC	UNIDROIT Principles of International Commercial Contracts

List of Abbreviations

Preface

This monograph is intended for the use of foreign lawyers desiring information about Swedish contract law.

Sweden does not have a comprehensive Civil Code like the Code Napoleon or the Bürgerliches Gesetzbuch. Instead, the Swedish civil law, and in particular contract law, has developed through piecemeal, ad hoc legislation, through the courts' adjudication and through scholarly legal work. The Swedish legal tradition is considered to belong neither to the civil law nor to the common law tradition but is rather seen as a methodological compromise between these two legal traditions. In the area of contract law the Swedish legal tradition is part of what is called the 'Nordic Legal Pragmatism' which stands for a rather pragmatic approach to, for instance, interpretation of contract.

The most important source of Swedish contract law is the Contracts Act of 1915. All of the Nordic countries have similar Contracts Acts and have developed similarly within contract law and, thus, sources of contract law from the other Nordic countries are relevant also in Sweden.

In writing this monograph we have relied on an extensive number of textbooks, articles, etc., by authoritative Nordic legal scholars. The references are found in the footnotes.

The monograph is up-to-date as of August 2014.

Boel Flodgren
Eric M. Runesson

General Introduction

§1. The General Background of the Country

I. Geography

1. Sweden, its formal name being The Kingdom of Sweden, is situated on the Scandinavian peninsula in Northern Europe, bordering Norway in the west, Finland in the north east and connected to Denmark in the south through the Öresund bridge. With regard to size, it is the third largest country in the European Union and the fifth largest in Europe. In terms of surface area it is comparable to Spain, Thailand and California. The length of the country from north to south is almost 1,600 kilometres which almost equals the distance from Malmö (in the south of Sweden) to Naples, Italy. More than half of the area is covered with forests and almost one tenth of the area consists of around 100,000 lakes.

2. The capital of Sweden is Stockholm with almost 900,000 inhabitants (more than 2 million living in the larger urban area of Stockholm). The second largest city is Gothenburg on the west coast (500,000 inhabitants, about 900,000 in the larger urban area) and the third largest city is Malmö in the south (300,000 inhabitants, about 650,000 in the larger urban area).

3. Sweden is rather sparsely populated with 23 inhabitants per square kilometre (EU average is 100 people per square kilometre). The population amounts to around 9,7 million people, 85% of whom living in urban areas and 23% of whom are younger than 20 years of age. About 16% of the population have been born in another country or have parents who were both born in another country (2014). The largest immigrant groups come from Finland, Iraq and Poland and more recently (figures from 2013) from Syria and Somalia.

II. Cultural Composition

4. Culturally, Sweden is, overall, a homogeneous country although a growing cultural influence from different immigrant groups can be noticed in the Swedish society. Since times immemorable, the indigenous Sami people have inhabited the north of Sweden. Today, the Sami people amounts to about 20,000 persons. There are five recognized national minorities, namely Jews, Roma, Sami, Swedish Finns and Tornedalers. The Swedish language is the recognized main language of the whole country. Together with Danish, Norwegian, Icelandic and Faroese, the Swedish language constitutes the Nordic part of the Germanistic language family. Long-established recognized minority languages are Yiddish, Romani Chib (all varieties); Sami (all varieties), Finnish and Meänkieli (Tornedal Finnish). Swedish minority policy covers all five of Sweden's national minorities. Common to these minority groups is that they have lived in Sweden for a long time and that they are groups with a distinct affinity. They also have their own religious, language or cultural affiliation and will to retain their identity.

III. Political History

5. Sweden has been an independent and a unified state since the Middle Ages. People have been living on Swedish land since 10,000–11,000 years b.Ch. During the early Middle Ages (between 800 and 1100) the Scandinavian Vikings became famous for their raids along the shores of the British Isles and the coastline of Western Europe. They were, however, not only cruel and brutal barbarians and fighters. They also appeared as peaceful traders; in fact, their strength to a large extent lay in their skill as traders and in their ability to settle new lands. They influenced the life, thought and language of Northern and Western Europe significantly. For instance, the English language is full of words which have Scandinavian roots, the word 'law' being one of them.

6. The Christian faith has been the state religion in Sweden since the Middle Ages and from the sixteenth century the Lutheran protestant faith is the dominant one. Today, Sweden is considered to be one of the most secular countries in the world. In the year 2000 the Church was completely separated from the state. However, the Christian culture and values are still strong fundaments underneath the Swedish society of today. Immigration has made the Muslim faith the second largest in Sweden.

7. Constitutionally Sweden is a monarchy, a system which in year 1544 became hereditary, starting with the Vasa family. Already in 1523 Gustavus I of the Vasa family was elected king over the independent state of Sweden (including Finland) and with him started the organization of a modern nation state and at this time Sweden also went through the Lutheran/protestant reformation of the Church. From the fifteenth century until 1809 Finland was part of the kingdom of Sweden. The southern part of Sweden and some territories in the north came under Swedish rule in the sixteenth century after having been conquered from Denmark-Norway. Successful warfare during the seventeenth century made Sweden expand geographically under what has come to be called the Grand Epoch. However, most of the conquered land outside the Scandinavian Peninsula was lost during the eighteenth and nineteenth centuries and with the death of King Charles XII in 1718 the Grand Epoch was definitely over and a parliamentary system started to develop, building on the four Estates, namely; nobility, clergy, burghers and peasants. The eastern part of Sweden, today Finland, was lost to Russia in 1809 and in the same year Sweden adopted a new Constitution creating a parliament consisting of the four Estates just mentioned, a system which continued until 1867.

8. Still in the beginning of the nineteenth century Sweden was a poor, sparsely populated country. From 1814 the country was in personal union with Norway (until then a part of Denmark) which was a compensation for the loss of Finland and a reward for having fought with the allies against Napoleon 1813–1814, but that union neither brought wealth nor was it ever a happy one and it was peacefully dissolved in 1905. Sweden has not been engaged in warfare since 1814. After that Sweden has adhered to a foreign policy based on non-alliance and neutrality. During the first and second world war Sweden took a neutral stand and Sweden stayed out of these wars. During the second world war, the price for staying outside was substantial concessions to Hitler–Germany in terms of extensive export of iron ore to Germany and the permission of the transportation of (unarmed) German soldiers across Swedish territory, particularly to Norway.

9. Sweden's development into a modern industrial state started at the end of the nineteenth century building mainly on its natural resources. The labour movement, consisting of an increasingly stronger trade union movement and the Social Democratic Party, started to grow at the end of the nineteenth century. From the 1930s, starting with the Social Democratic Governments, Sweden's development towards a modern 'welfare state' began. Free public education (also at the university level), a national health system, generous parental leave provisions and extensive day-care services for small children as well as a national old age care system are some of the services provided by the state/municipalities in exchange for high taxes, mainly in the form of VAT and income tax. Privatization of public services (education, health care, old age care) is rapidly taking place in the new millennium.

10. Full male suffrage was introduced in 1911 and universal suffrage (also including women) was established in 1919 and was used for the first time in the general parliamentary election in 1921. A mandatory municipal school system introduced in the 1840s contributed efficiently to eliminate illiteracy.

IV. Political System

11. Sweden is a constitutional monarchy with a democratic parliamentary system. Parliamentary elections take place every fourth year and the same is true for the municipal elections and the elections to the regional council, the so-called landstinget, Region Skania and Region West. The Parliament which is called 'Riksdag' is a unicameral legislature with 349 members. The functions of the Riksdag are found in the Instrument of Government (Sw: *Regeringsformen*). The seat of the Riksdag is in Stockholm. Furthermore, Sweden is a member of the European Union since 1 January 1995.

12. Between 1932 and 2006 the Socialdemocratic Party was in power except for a period of nine years. Since 2006 Sweden has a liberal-conservative government.

V. Economy

13. Sweden is a small open economy, heavily dependent on international trade. Almost 2/3 of the Swedish GNP comes from trade in goods. In the 1950s and 1960s the Swedish economy expanded rapidly. One important reason for this was the fact that Sweden had not been part of the second world war which gave Swedish industry a competitive advantage after the war. Other reasons for the rapid economic development were the growing labour forces and substantial investments in education and infrastructure during the decades after the war. Around the 1970s Sweden had its peak of economic development and was ranked fourth in the OECD welfare league, measuring GDP, after the US, Switzerland and Luxemburg. In the 1970s and 1990s the Swedish economy was subject to severe crises and since then the Swedish industry has been through deep structural changes.

14. While in the 1970s, textile, food, wood and pulp made up for major parts of the Swedish industry, in this millennium the picture has changed to an industry also producing things such as minerals, machinery and transport equipment, electronics and telecommunication equipment, energy products, advanced paper products and special steel and chemicals, i.e., products of a more knowledge intensive character. Whole industries of what were in the 1970s important branches for the Swedish economy such as shipbuilding have completely disappeared. After the second world war Swedish export of both goods and services has substantially increased and makes up today for about half of Swedish GDP which is twice as high as the world average. More than 70% of the value of the Swedish export of goods goes to European countries whereas import from Europe amounts to 84% (of which 69% comes from EU (28)) of the total import. The overall most important trading partners (2014) are Germany, Norway, Great Britain, Denmark, Finland and the USA.

15. Another result of the structural changes of the Swedish economy is the increasing importance of the service sector; today at least 75% of the Swedish labour force works in the service sector and services make up for 28% of the total export. Swedish foreign direct investment and other countries' foreign direct investment in Sweden are also important to study in order to understand Sweden's role in international trade and how it depends on international supply chains and corporate structures. To an increasing extent Swedish firms establish subsidiaries in other countries from which platforms they produce and distribute goods and services. Foreign investors have made significant investments in Sweden during the last decades by buying large Swedish companies but after the financial crisis in 2008 foreign direct investment in Sweden has decreased.

16. A significant characteristic of Swedish industry is the relatively large amount of large companies. Sweden has around ten of the world's 500 largest companies and a dozen in the second largest category. This gives strength in export trade and also helps smaller companies to be exposed to the world market. Especially the high-technology based companies participate fully in the global economy.

17. Another imperative feature of the Swedish industry is its international character. Sweden belongs to the most internationalized countries when it comes to foreign ownership of companies situated in Sweden and to Swedish ownership of companies abroad. Since 2004 the amount of employees abroad in Swedish multinational companies was almost twice the number of employees of the same companies in Sweden.

18. Today, studies of Sweden often arrive at the conclusion, on the positive end, that Sweden ranks high when comes to IT, gender equality and the environment. On the negative end, Sweden is ranked low for its high income taxes and its relatively slow pace of innovation and its rather inflexible labour market structure.

VI. Legal Culture and Legal System

19. The Swedish legal system belongs to the continental European tradition, what is usually called the civil law tradition. Reminiscences from Roman law are clearly identifiable in the structure and underlying principles of the Swedish legal system. From modern times the German influence has been significant, particularly in private law. Sweden (then including Finland) adopted a national code in 1734, a code which formally is still in force. Materially, there are only a few enactments left from that time. Efforts have been made to legislate a whole new national code, but that effort has not been successful. Instead, the material content of the Swedish national code of 1734 has been gradually renewed and replaced throughout the years.

20. Beginning in 1872 there has been close legislative cooperation between the Nordic countries, particularly in family law, contract law, intellectual property law and torts. Since the 1960s this cooperation is no longer that intense, even if there is still a certain level of legislative cooperation among the Nordic countries.

21. According to the Swedish Constitution, Instrument of Government (Regeringsformen), Chapter 1, section 1, paragraph 3 'the public power should be executed under the enacted statutes (in Swedish "lagarna")'. This means that these texts, the statutes that have been enacted by Parliament (Riksdagen), have a unique status as a source of law in Sweden.

22. Furthermore, according to the Swedish Constitution, 'the public power shall be exercised with respect for the equal value of all human beings and for each individual person's freedom and dignity' (Regeringsformen (Instrument of Government), Chapter 1, section 1, paragraph 1). Since 1995 the European Convention for the Protection of Human Rights and the Fundamental Freedoms is adopted as Swedish law. The values expressed in these documents are an essential part of the Swedish legal system and shall influence the way Swedish law is interpreted and applied. The Swedish Constitution regulates which institution has the power to enact the different types of legislative acts that constitute the Swedish legal system.

23. International conventions/treaties entered into by the Swedish government do not become part of Swedish law until they have been transformed into Swedish law through an enactment decision by Parliament. In 1994 Sweden transformed the law of the European Union into national Swedish law, entering into force 1 January 1995. In other words, since 1 January 1995, Sweden is a member of the European Union. Thus, European Union legislation, mainly regulations, directives and decisions, as well as the rules established by the European Court of Justice, are important sources of Swedish law.

24. There is no strict hierarchy of the sources of law, nevertheless, with regard to how the law ought to be interpreted, there is consensus amongst legal scholars, judges and practising lawyers as to how legal reasoning should be performed. The most important sources of law are the written statutes in the form of constitutional acts (grundlagar) and ordinary acts (lagar), i.e., the legislation enacted by the Swedish parliament (Riksdagen). Even ordinances (förordningar) enacted by the government are considered authoritative sources of law. Since the legislative process is rather structured and formalized, the legislative preparatory works of the statute (*travaux préparatoires*, in Swedish: *förarbeten*) is considered an important source of law for the identification of the content of the statute with the pronouncement of the responsible minister and the report of the relevant standing committee of the Riksdag being the most important. The *travaux préparatoires* are often followed, but they are not formally binding. In addition – and this is where the Swedish legal system resembles the common law – precedent, i.e., decisions by the courts at the top of the court system (Supreme Court, Supreme Administrative Court, the Labour Court and the Market Court), although not formally binding, are also considered important sources of law in Sweden, more so than in other clear-cut civil law or code based systems. It is generally considered that precedent should be followed by the lower courts. In certain areas of private law, mercantile usages and customs play the role of sources of law.

25. Furthermore, there are various sources that may be taken into account, such as authoritative legal doctrine, and various forms of soft law instruments, such as recommendations and directives issued by public authorities or relevant private organizations.

26. Moreover, Sweden has a three level court system. The system is divided between the general courts (handling civil and criminal matters), administrative courts (handling matters in which a public authority is a party, among other things, tax cases) and a few so-called special courts, for instance the Labour Court. The Supreme Court and the Supreme Administrative Court only give certiorari in which (a) it is important that a general ruling be given by way of precedent for judicial practice or (b) special reasons exist, such as a grave mistake made by the lower court. Swedish courts frequently use the system of dissenting opinions.

§2. Swedish Law Belongs to the Nordic Legal Family

27. Swedish civil law builds on the civil law tradition with roots in Roman law. A Civil Code defining the overall system, the general principles, the concepts, etc., of civil law does not exist in Sweden. Statutory regulation is relatively scarce in the field of contract law and only a few of all different types of contracts are subject to special legislation. This leaves wide space for the application of general principles of law. Thus, court cases and legal doctrine are important sources of contract law in Sweden like in the rest of the Nordic countries. The lack of regulation has contributed to a rather pragmatic and flexible contract law. Within the legal family system, Swedish contract law of today is considered to belong neither to the continental civil law tradition, nor to the common law tradition. The Nordic legal tradition is rather seen as a compromise between these two dominant legal traditions. The Nordic tradition has been labelled Nordic Legal Pragmatism which puts emphasis on the rather flexible and pragmatic approach of Nordic contract law with regard to, for instance, interpretation of contract.

§3. Primacy of Legislation

28. It is correct to say that Swedish law consists primarily of rules enacted by the parliament in the form of parliamentary acts (Sw: *lag*). The parliament may confer upon the government the authority to issue regulations (Sw: *förordning*) within specific areas. See Chapter 8 of the Constitutional Act (Sw: *Regeringsformen* 1974:152), The government can in turn confer upon governmental authorities to issue instructions regarding the details in such regulations (Sw: *föreskrift*). Parliamentary acts, regulations and instructions are often generally referred to as legislation and it is said that the legislation is an expression of the will of the legislator. The legislator would rather express the underlying policies of the legislation in preparatory works such as governmental bills (Sw: *proposition*) which are often preceded by official reports on the subject of the legislation (Sw: *statlig utredning*). The preparatory works often note that the intended legislation does not purport to solve all problems and that upcoming issues will have to be solved through judge made law (Sw: *rättstillämpningen*). In this sense it can be said that legislation has primacy in principle, although much of the law is left to the judicature, which in turn to a large extent will be influenced by the policies expressed in the preparatory works. Typically, a judge would strive to find out the underlying purposes of any piece of legislation and try to further those purposes when creating a solution for problems not directly addressed in the legislation. This approach is characterized as the teleological method.

§4. The Role of the Judiciary

29. Constitutionally, Swedish courts are independent of the political system, i.e., Parliament, the Government and public authorities (Chapter 11, section 2 of the Instrument of Government). The general court system in Sweden (Sw: *de allmänna domstolarna*) is a three level system with district courts (around 60), 6 courts of appeal and one Supreme Court. The general courts handle both civil and criminal cases. The decisions by the Supreme Court are important sources of law, although, formally, lower courts are not bound to follow the decisions by the Supreme Court. Judges are appointed by the Government and enjoy a high degree of employment protection as an expression of the recognition of the constitutional principle of the 'division of powers'.

30. There are sixteen judges on the Supreme Court. They work in divisions and usually five judges constitute the court in regular cases. In principle, the Supreme Court is bound to follow its earlier judgments but if it intends to change an earlier judgment, all of the Supreme Court judges shall participate in the decision (*plenum*). In most matters there is a requirement for certiorari (Sw: *prövningstillstånd*) for a case to be admitted to the Supreme Court. The same is true for the courts of appeal, but here the admission is more generous. In criminal cases in the lower courts there are lay judges functioning as judges together with the legally trained judges. The lay judges vote in matters of fact and matters of law.

31. There is a special administrative court system for cases in which one of the parties is a public authority. These cases often start with a public authority making a decision affecting a citizen or a legal person who then appeals the decision, for instance a decision regarding taxation. There is a three level court system consisting of the administrative district court (Sw: *länsrätt*), the administrative court of appeal (Sw: *kammarrätt*) and the Supreme Administrative Court (Sw: *Högsta förvaltningsdomstolen*).

32. Furthermore, a few specialized courts with special jurisdiction exist in certain areas. Among these could be mentioned the Labour Court (Sw: *arbetsdomstolen*), the Market Court (Sw: *marknadsdomstolen*) and the environmental court system where there is a special Land and Environmental Court of Appeal in the form of a general Appeals court acting with the addition of technical judges (Sw: *mark- och miljööverdomstolen*).

§5. BETWEEN PUBLIC AND PRIVATE LAW ('ADMINISTRATIVE CONTRACTS')

33. There is no clear distinction in Swedish law between private and administrative contracts such as in e.g., French law. The courts for civil matters are competent to adjudicate disputes between private entities and state or public authorities. In doing so, the courts will have regard to whether the application or interpretation of the contract should be influenced by a public law context so that ordinary contract principles ought not to apply[1] regarding a contract between a private person and a municipality and the question of whether the municipality had the right to payment under an agreement to provide child care notwithstanding the fact that performance of the services was impeded by a strike. The court found that the legal

1. See e.g., the Supreme Court case NJA 2008 p. 642.

relationship was of a public law nature but that the private law aspects dominated when it came to determining the payment obligations under the contract.

§6. Distinction between Civil Law and Commercial Law ('Commercial Contracts')

34. There is no clear distinction in Swedish law between civil law and commercial law. Legislation in a field of law applies to all actors, although consumers may enjoy mandatory rights under consumer legislation. Thus, the provisions in the Contracts Act (Sw: *Avtalslagen* 1915:218) apply to transactions between private persons and to transactions between commercial actors alike. Likewise, the Sale of Goods Act (Sw: *Köplagen* 1990:931) applies to all sales of goods transactions although the provisions of the Consumer Sales Act (Sw: *Konsumentköplagen* 1990:932) takes precedence in transactions between consumers and commercial sellers.

Introduction to the Law of Contracts

§1. Definition of Contract

35. There is no definition of contract to be found in the Contracts Act and the attempt to describe rather than define the concept which was made in the preparatory works from 1914 is based on the concept of a declaration of will for the purpose of establishing, changing or terminating a legal relationship. To be relevant as the basis for a contract the declaration of will must be appreciable to a receiver. It turns out that the concept of a declaration of will is not well suited to describe what a contract is – or rather what constitutes a contract – for it is the extrinsically appreciable phenomena (such as words as well as signs and actions) that count provided that they from an objective standpoint are such that the receiver has reason to believe that they are an expression of a will to contract and thus accepted.[2]

I. Will, Intent and Reliance

36. The three concepts *will*, *intent* and *reliance* play an important role in contract law, particularly when the parties have a dispute with regard to what they have actually agreed in their contract. The main source to consult when trying to resolve such a contractual dispute is, of course, the contract itself. The contract is understood as the joint will of the parties (Sw: '*gemensamma partsviljan*'), expressed as two 'declarations of will for the purpose of establishing, changing or terminating a legal relationship' as it is expressed in the preparatory work to the Contracts Act. The 'will' is therefore a crucial concept in contract law (Sw: *viljeteorin*); if in a dispute, the common will of the parties at the time of the conclusion of the contract can be proved, that means that the content of the contract is clarified. Another concept, akin to will, is intent/intention; the (common) intention of the parties is what determines the content of the contract. Since it is usually difficult in a dispute to clarify the will/intent/intention of the parties at the time of the conclusion of the contract, if the other party did not know or could not have been unaware of what the intent was, the intent of a party is instead often clarified according to *the reliance theory/the principle of justified reliance* (Sw: *tillitsteorin/den befogade tillitens princip*). This means that the conclusion regarding what constitutes a party's

2. See Adlercreutz & Gorton, Avtalsrätt I, pp 24 et seq. (2011). (Cit. Adlercreutz&Gorton I).

intent, is drawn from that party's statements and conduct and other relevant circumstances, as those would have been perceived of and understood by a reasonable person of the same kind in the same circumstances. The will/intent is not seen as matter of what that particular party actually intended, the *subjective method* (since this is mostly impossible to find out), but instead the intent is seen as something which could be found from a more generalized way of reasoning, the *objective method*. The justified reliance is a predominant concept in today's contract law, particularly in contract interpretation but also, in rare cases, with repercussions for a contract party's liability vis-à-vis third parties (NJA 1987 p. 692).

II. Freedom of Contract

37. Freedom of contract prevails of old as a fundamental principle of Swedish contract law. This means that legally capable parties are free to conclude a contract and shape its contents subject to mandatory rules and public policy.

38. The freedom of contract principle is based on the premises that the parties are acting with free will and with access to adequate information. When the free will premise fails the contract is considered fundamentally flawed. The classic rules on invalidity due to e.g., duress (Contracts Act sections 28–29), fraud (Contract Act section 30) or usury (section 31) can be cited as examples of situations when a contract is not upheld due to the view that one of the parties is deemed not to have acted with free will.

39. The same policy underpins section 36 of the Contracts Act; a provision that provides for adjustment/modification or the setting aside of unreasonable contract terms *inter alia* due to the circumstances under which the contract was concluded (lack of will) or due to the contract provisions as such (lack of information or understanding).

40. Section 36 of the Act was introduced in 1976 and has had most of its impact in consumer contracts and is now to be applied in conjunction with section 11 of the Act (1979:417) on Consumer Contract Conditions, which was introduced in the process of implementing the Council Directive 93/13/EEC of 5 April 1993 on unfair terms in consumer contracts. The provision is restrictively used in commercial contracts, but it can be assumed that the provision has had some preventive impact[3] regarded a clause that gave one party (a bank) the right to unilaterally change the conditions of a letter of credit (allowing the bank to accept that the seller replaced the goods with other goods). The clause was considered to be at odds with general practices in the bank sector and the clause was set aside.[4] On a general note it can be said that the more a condition deviates from non-mandatory rules or prevailing

3. NJA 1983 p. 332.
4. An odd case regards the setting aside of an arbitration clause; NJA 1979 p. 666. Compare however NJA 1992 p. 290 and NJA 1992 p. 143.

practices in one party's interest, the likelier it is that the clause may be stricken out or adjusted as unreasonable.

III. Binding Character of Contract

41. A contract can be explained as binding since the parties want to be bound or, with a reliance based theory, because the receiver of a statement that appears as a declaration of a will to be bound needs to be able to believe in the appearance and act accordingly. Some would rather explain that a contract is binding because it follows from the nature of things; contracts are binding as balls are round.[5] Nevertheless, the *pacta sunt servanda* principle may in exceptional cases yield to rules that can be traced back to the opposing *clausula rebus sic stantibus* principle. This can be the case when there is an *error in motivis* under the doctrine of failed assumptions (Sw: *förutsättningsläran*) provided that the promisee is considered closer to bear the risk for the mistake than the promisor. Thus, it may be that the effect of unforeseen circumstances can make it reasonable to release one of the parties from the contract or lead to adjustment under the Contracts Act section 36.[6] The indexation (relative to the price of wheat) of fees payable under a forty-nine year tenancy agreement was adjusted due to inflation. The doctrine of failed assumptions can also serve as a compliment to the statutory rules on invalidity due to lack of will. This can be the case when the promisee has caused a mistake in motives.[7] A seller who delivered goods to the buyer was entitled to take repossession of the goods notwithstanding the buyer's bankruptcy due to the doctrine of failed assumptions, since the buyer had acted so as to diminish the seller's appreciation of the bankruptcy risk.[8] Purchase of condominium apartment upheld in spite of failed assumptions.

42. Beyond these general observations, it should be noted that a contract can be modified as a result of *naturalia negotii.* An example is that a seller's promise to deliver can be modified and turned into a claim for damages in so far as the delivery would lead to costs that are disproportionate in comparison with the buyer's interest to claim specific performance.[9] Likewise, a seller's interest to continue specific performance may yield to the interest of the buyer to stop the performance and cancel with damage liability.[10] Swedish law here seems to be in between legal systems that in principle require specific performance unless performance is impossible and legal systems that treat specific performance as an outflow of the law of equity.

5. See Hellner, *Rättsteori*, pp 117 et seq.
6. See NJA 1983 p. 385.
7. See e.g., NJA 1985 p. 178.
8. See however NJA 1997 p. 5.
9. See s. 23 Sale of Goods Act.
10. See s. 52 Sale of Goods Act.

IV. Mandatory Rules

43. Mandatory rules limit the exercise of free will. The introduction of mandatory rules may be motivated by a perceived need to protect public policy. In such cases the state will not recognize or enforce the contract because it is considered to be unworthy of legal protection *(pactum turpe)* or actions *contra bonos mores*. See e.g., Svea Court of Appeals, RH 2004:41 regarding non-enforcement of a promise to pay a woman for carrying out an abortion. An agreement that directly aims at tax evasion by means of misinforming the tax authority was declared invalid according to 'general principles of law'.[11] Likewise, a promise to settle a gambling debt is generally considered not to be enforceable and claims for repayment would in principle be denied. The Supreme Court has taken a cautious approach to impose invalidity on moral grounds.[12] Claim for repayment of stakes to an organizer of a poker tournament was granted when the tournament was interrupted and the stakes were seized for the organizer's debt to a third party. The outcome was partly motivated by the avoidance of unjust enrichment, but has been characterized as an outflow of a pragmatic approach.[13]

44. Public policy consideration may also lead to that certain monopoly holders or parties that are licensed to operate by the state are deemed to be under a duty to contract. Similarly, the public interest to control the use of real property rights can give rise to preemptive rights for an affected municipality. The same interest underpins requirements for permission to sell certain kinds of real property (apartment buildings and agricultural estates).

45. Likewise, a duty to contract may follow indirectly from non-discrimination policies and a refusal to contract may even be criminal.[14]

46. A large part of mandatory rules are paternalistic in the sense that typically weak parties are deemed to need protection from their own decision to agree to certain provisions. It can also be said that such parties do not act with free will (or an adequate understanding of the consequences of their actions) or are dependent on the relation to the other party. This has motivated a number of mandatory rules in consumer legislation, lease agreements and labour law but also in commercial contracts such as commercial agency (implementing the directive 86/653/EEC) and insurance law.

47. Swedish law also accepts limitations to the freedom of the parties to shape their contract due to the policy to further efficient competition and takes the position that agreements that in a noticeable way distort or limit competition are null and void.

---

11. NJA 1992 p. 299.
12. see NJA 1997 p. 93, 2002 p. 332 and 2004 p. 682. See also NJA 1989 p. 768.
13. See Adlercreutz & Gorton I, p. 298.
14. See Ch. 16 s. 9 of the Penal Code. Compare The Non-discrimination Act (2008:567).

48. When a mandatory statutory provision does not stipulate the effect if the parties try to set aside the provision, the effect will be determined by the court. The Supreme Court in NJA 1997 p. 93 has held that the effect will depend on whether invalidity is required considering the purpose of the mandatory rule and the effect of invalidity on parties acting in good faith. Invalidity is declared ex officio.

V. Rights 'In Personam' and Rights 'In Rem'

49. Swedish Contract Law uses a similar distinction as between right in personam (Sw: *obligatorisk rättighet*) and right in rem (Sw: *sakrätt*). A right in personam can only be exercised against the person who has given rise to the right, whereas a right in rem can be exercised against third persons. Rights in rem do not fall within the area of contract law, but are instead studied in property law.[15] It should be noted however that many statutes that primarily regard the rights in personam of the parties may contain provisions that regard the rights in rem. An example is section 54 of the Sale of Goods Act; a seller may not terminate a contract if the goods have been passed on to the buyer (who by taking possession of the goods becomes the owner), unless the seller has retained ownership (or the right to terminate) according to a provision in the agreement. Such provisions may however be ineffective against third parties, e.g., the buyer's bankruptcy estate.[16]

§2. Historical Background of the Law of Contracts

I. Influence of Roman Law

50. Roman law provides the original basis for Swedish contract law although European continental law, particularly German law, has been the 'agent' with the help of which Roman law concepts and principles have been transplanted into Swedish law. In 1686 king Carl XI appointed a Law Commission with the aim of organizing the Swedish law. The Law Commission's work resulted in the coming into being of Sweden's first comprehensive statute book in 1734. There was no particular regulation about contracts but commercial issues were dealt with in the special commercial chapter (*Handelsbalken*) which in the following presentation will be called 'the Commercial Code'. Sweden has never had a special Commercial Law Codex, i.e., a comprehensive Commercial Code, nor any special Civil Law Codex (a comprehensive Civil Code). In the beginning of the nineteenth century the law had grown and become fragmented and a new effort to create a comprehensive Swedish Civil Code was made through the appointment in 1811 of a Law Committee with this task. In 1826 the committee put forward a proposal for a Civil Code which had the Code Napoleon as a model. If the statute book of 1734 expressed the values and the structure of the old medieval society, this proposal advocated a liberal world order with autonomous economic and legal actors. The free will of such

15. See s. 6 further below.
16. See Part II Ch. 4.

autonomous actors should be the constituting factor for the civil law and extensive freedom of contract was seen as a leading principle. There was fierce criticism from the part of judges and lawyers of this proposal and it never took the form of a Civil Law Codex. Since then, Sweden has only had piecemeal, ad hoc legislation within the area of civil law. The development of the civil law in Sweden, thus, has mainly been the result of the courts' adjudication (Sw: *praxis*) and of scholarly legal work (Sw: *doktrin*) which means that Swedish civil law rests on a plurality of sources. The Swedish legal tradition is considered to belong neither to the continental civil law tradition, nor to the common law tradition. The Scandinavian legal tradition is rather seen as a methodological compromise between these two other dominant legal traditions. In the area of contract law, the Swedish legal tradition is part of what is called the 'Nordic Legal Pragmatism' which is characterized by a rather flexible approach to, for instance, interpretation of contracts.

51. Swedish contract law took the shape of legislation in the Contracts Act of 1915 (still in force). This legislation relied heavily on German contract law which in turn was and is embedded in Roman law. The Swedish legislative work leading to the Contracts Act took place in close cooperation with Denmark and Norway which led to the enactment of almost identical Contracts Acts in these three Nordic countries in the beginning of the twentieth century (Sweden 1915, Denmark 1917 and Norway 1918). Finland enacted a similar legislation in 1929.

52. In Roman law there were no general rules about contract that applied to all types of contracts; this is a much later idea. In Roman law transactions were valid only if they fitted into and were performed according to the rules that regulated the different types of contract. This concept of contract was inherited by Swedish contract law and was expressed in the Swedish statute book of 1734. In its Commercial Code specific types of contract, for instance the sales contract, were regulated but there were no general rules regarding how a contract would become binding, when a contract was not valid, etc. This meant that if a transaction or an agreement did not fit into any of the regulated types of contract, it simply was not a legally valid contract or the transaction lead to legal consequences that did not meet the intentions of the parties. This system became a strait-jacket which prevented economic development.[17]

53. Gradually, beginning at the end of the nineteenth century, this formal way of looking on contract law was abandoned and the idea of a general contract law, i.e., distinguishing rules that would apply to all types of contracts and bringing them together systematically into a general contract law, started to take hold. With the adoption of the Contracts Act of 1915, Sweden got its first general contract law. This meant that the general issues of when a contract becomes binding, when a contract is not valid, etc. were established as a special body of law, in Sweden referred to as general contract law (Sw: *allmän avtalsrätt*). When Swedish lawyers talk about 'the special contract law' they usually refer to the part of contract law which deals with the different contract types and the different types of obligations that those create

17. See Adlercreutz & Gorton I, p. 32.

between the parties. Today one finds a high degree of flexibility when it comes to the characterization of a contract and new contract types are constantly emerging in response to the development of new forms of economic relationships and exchanges in industry and society at large.

II. Later Development of Swedish Contract Law

54. Swedish contract law has developed along the lines of international contract law. This means, for instance, that there has been a move away from the more subjective way of looking at the contract, emphasizing the will of the parties as the decisive factor, towards a more objective way of looking at the contract where the legitimate expectations of a reasonable person is recognized as the decisive factor when it comes to deciding the content of the contract. Furthermore, the principle of good faith and fair dealing which in Swedish law is labelled 'the loyalty principle', is gradually being recognized as a general principle of our contract law, particularly in long-time contract relationships. The interpretation principle expressed in CISG Article 7.1 is often referred to as a general principle, not only for interpretation, but for the contract relationship as a whole. Even if not formally binding, Article 1.7(1) of UNIDROIT Principles which puts on the parties a duty to act according to 'good faith and fair dealing' in international commercial contracts can also be regarded as a general principle recognized under Swedish domestic law.

55. In Swedish contract law, as in the contract law of most other countries, one can distinguish between rules that are 'repressive', i.e., rules that hinder and forbids certain actions and ways to behave in contractual relations, on the one hand, and rules that are 'productive', i.e., rules that are conducive to the intentions of the parties and function as 'oil in the machinery' for transactions and agreements of different types, on the other hand. The first type of rules are usually *mandatory*, or 'immutable' rules, which means that they cannot be set aside by contractual agreement, whereas the second type belongs to the type of rules called *default rules,* which means that the parties to the contract can set them aside and agree otherwise. Default rules – if not set aside by contract – play the role of gap-filling in incomplete contracts. The idea behind making some rules mandatory is that the legislator wants to protect the parties within the contract or parties outside the contract.

56. The principle of offer and acceptance and the idea of the offer/promise being of binding character during a certain period of time, were acknowledged in Swedish contract law during the nineteenth century. In earlier times, when it was unusual for buyer and seller to be at a distance from each other, there had not been much need for any other principle than the contract principle, i.e., that nothing was binding on the parties until they had both agreed to the contract.

57. The development of contract law during the end of the nineteenth century took the form of a separation between sales law and contract law, and a special Sale of Goods Act was enacted at the beginning of the twentieth century, entering into force in 1905. After that, the Contracts Act was enacted in 1915 and entered into force in 1916. This Act, still in force, contains only general contract law issues, i.e., it does not deal with contractual obligations but only with general issues pertaining to all types of contracts, such as formation of contract, agency and invalidity. It was never meant to regulate all issues pertaining to, for instance, formation of contract but mainly the issue of formation through correspondence, i.e., contract *inter absentes*.[18]

58. In Swedish contract law the discussion regarding whether the contract law should build on the promissory principle or on the contract principle was solved by the Contracts Act according to which a promise is binding for the offeror once it has reached the offeree.

§3. Classification of Contracts

I. Consensual Contracts

59. Consensual contract are agreements which the parties have entered into by free will and which become binding because the parties intended to be bound. Hence, consensual contracts are not subject to any formal requirements.

II. Solemn Contracts

60. Some contracts require the observance of a formal writing requirement, but there is no parallel to a requirement for contracts to be drawn up by a notary that can be seen in other jurisdictions.

III. Real Contracts

61. Real contracts become binding not by the exchange of an offer and an acceptance, but by the performance (delivery of money or property). Examples are rare and limited to gratuitous transactions.

IV. Bilateral and Unilateral Contracts

62. A bilateral, or synallagmatic, contract creates reciprocal obligations. The concept is mainly used when determining one party's right to withhold his performance. Unilateral contract creates obligations only on one side of the agreement. It should be noted that Swedish law does not require anything equivalent to consideration.

---

18. See A. Adlercreutz, Högsta domsmakten i Sverige under 200 år. Del 2. Högsta domstolen och civilrätten, p. 30, (1989).

V. Onerous and Gratuitous Contracts

63. Onerous contracts impose obligation on both sides of a contract. Thus, onerous contracts are bilateral. Gratuitous contracts (Sw: *benefika avtal*) are meant to confer an advantage on one party without reciprocity. Examples include gifts and interest free loans. Acceptance as a requirement for binding effect is typically replaced by performance by the obligor. In determining the effect of gratuitous contracts, there is a tendency to have more regard to the will of the obligor than the reliance of the obligee.[19] Changed circumstances may also be of relevance and operate to relieve the obligor of his obligations.[20] If the economic situation of the donor worsens before the gift is completed the donor may be released from his promise or the gift be reduced.[21]

64. Semi-gratuitous contracts, i.e., onerous contracts where the benefits provided by one party are intended not to correspond to the benefits provided by the other party are generally seen as gratuitous and are referred to as *remuneratoriska avtal*.

VI. Commutative and Aleatory Contracts

65. The distinction between commutative and aleatory contracts is rarely made. In commutative contracts the quantum of the performances on both sides of the contract is determined from the outset. Aleatory contracts on the other hand are characterized by an element of chance that can make the quantum variable as the case is when a buyer buys the next year's crop from the seller.

VII. Intuitu Personae Contracts

66. Intuitu personae contracts refer to agreements where the personal qualities of one of the parties are of the essence. The concept of intuitu personae contract is however rarely used in the discourse. Typically, such a contract comes to an end by the death of the obligor.[22] Also, the obligee cannot transfer his rights to a third person as far as his personal qualities are deemed to have been essential for the obligor's will to conclude the contract.

VIII. Nominate and Innominate Contracts

67. Nominate contract refer to contract types that are subject to statutory rules, such as sales contracts, agency or gifts. Innominate contracts refer to contract types

19. Compare Adlercreutz & Gorton I, p. 276.
20. See e.g., the Gift Act (1936:83) s. 5.
21. Compare s. 1 III above.
22. See e.g., Ch. 2 s. 26 of the Partnership Act (1980:1102).

that are of a younger date and not systematically dealt with in statutory law, such as leasing and licensing contracts. Innominate contracts are frequently referred to as contracts *sui generis*.

IX. Standard Form Contracts

68. Standard form contracts are usually divided into adhesion contracts and agreed documents. Adhesion contracts are drawn up by one party – typically with strong bargaining power. Agreed documents are typically negotiated between organizations representing the interests of all parties concerned.

X. Main Contracts and Accessory Contracts

69. When the existence of a contract is necessarily linked to another contract, the first contract is referred to as an accessory contract and the latter referred to as the main contract. An example of an accessory contract is suretyship. If the main contract is void, the suretyship is also void.

XI. Frame Contracts

70. Frame contracts create a frame for later contracts. E.g., a distributor's contract provides a framework for later sales contracts between the supplier and the distributor. It should be noted that the frame contract and a subsequent contract for sales in principle are deemed as two separate legal relationships.

§4. Contract and Torts

71. The common law concept of 'tort', building historically on the concept of 'action', is not found in Swedish law even if the term is used, particularly in comparative contexts. Rather, in Swedish law, rules regarding non-contractually based liability rest on the idea of 'delict' and have their origin in criminal law. If a person negligently (or intentionally) inflicts harm on another person with whom he has no contractual relationship, the injured person has a right to compensation from the injuring person (the 'tortfeasor'). This situation gives rise to 'an action in tort' for the injured party, i.e., he has the right to be compensated for the harm. If strict liability applies, the right to compensation follows from the mere causing of the injury; no intention or negligence has to be proved. Conceptually, there is no sharp line between contractual liability and torts. However, textbooks usually treat mainly the one or the other, i.e., either contractually based compensation rules, or liability in tort.[23] The law of torts is closely connected to insurance law. Thus, issues regarding personal injury and damaged property are usually matters dealt with in actions of

23. See Hellner-Radetzki, Skadeståndsrätt, p. 27 (8 ed, 2010) [cit. Hellner & Radetzki].

tort/insurance law, whereas compensation for economic loss is more often a matter of action in contract, since actions for recovery of pure economic loss are in principle not possible in torts (see below).

72. The Tort Liability Act provides the general basis and principles for damages in torts and contract. The Act's provisions are basically default rules which means that they can be set aside through contract, e.g., with an exemption clause.

73. There are however differences between tortious and contractual liability both with regard to the prerequisites for liability and with regard to the way compensation is calculated.

74. The general prerequisite for damage liability in tort law is negligence, whereas the prerequisites for damage liability in contract law varies depending on the type of contract and the type of loss. For instance, a party to a sales contract is in principle strictly liable for the economic loss caused by a breach, but only insofar as the loss can be characterized as direct. For indirect losses the same prerequisite as used in tort law applies; i.e., negligence.[24]

75. Pure economic loss is in principle not recoverable in tort unless supported by special provisions in statutory law or the loss resulted from a criminal offence. However, the requirements for compensation for pure economic loss have been loosened up somewhat during later years.[25] In cases of injuries inflicted through gross negligence, the courts have shown an inclination to construct contractual-like relationships between the injured and the injuring party in order to make it possible to compensate for the injured person's pure economic loss.[26]

76. The question whether an injured person should have the right to choose between an action in tort or in contract, when both kinds of actions are conceivable is unclear in Swedish law.

77. There are two opposing views on the Swedish law in this respect. One is that a person who is bound by a contract should not be deprived of the right to compensation which he would have had, had there been no contract; in other words, an action in tort should always be an alternative also for a contractually bound party. The other argument goes as follows. If two parties have agreed in a contract which rules should prevail between them, it should not be possible to circumvent these rules by claiming compensation under an action in tort. It is unclear which one of these arguments actually prevail in Sweden.[27] However, the content of the Swedish law on this point seems to be that the injured person is not entitled to bring an action in tort instead of an action in contract on the mere ground that this is more advantageous for him (ibid.). A similar question is whether a contractually bound party

24. See further Part II Ch. 4.
25. See Hellner & Radetzki, pp 67–78.
26. See Hellner & Radetzki, p. 75 and NJA 1987 p. 692 and NJA 2005 p. 608.
27. See Hellner & Radetzki, p. 96.

can avoid the effects of an exemption clause or a clause limiting his liability by bringing an action in tort, i.e., a non-contractually based claim, not vis-à-vis his contract party but vis-à-vis the contract party's party. This is probably possible only in exceptional cases.[28] Later case law has limited the possibility to direct a claim vis-à-vis the contract party's party at least in the case of 'contract chains' where the different contracts contain similar liability clauses.[29]

78. The underlying idea of the right to compensation is that the injured person shall be economically compensated to the extent where he is put back into the same economic situation in which he would have been had the harm not been inflicted on him. For contractually based claims this means that he should be entitled to the expectation interest, i.e., what he would have earned if the contract had been performed accordingly. The amount of compensation can be difficult to calculate and prove for the plaintiff. If this is the case the court can assess the loss to a reasonable amount.[30] Often the right to compensation is regulated in the contract in the form of liquidated damages, for instance in a sales contract, amounting to a percentage of the price.

§5. Contract and Quasi-contracts

79. The concept of quasi contract is not a legally defined concept in Swedish law and it seems to be used in different ways in different jurisdictions. In Sweden, the concept has been used for a long time (going back at least to the beginning of the nineteenth century). The concept has been used by the courts as a means to move the borders of what is basically non-contractual relationships into what is called 'contract like' relationships, thereby creating contractually based liability for the party who is considered to have acted negligently and thereby caused the harm.[31]

80. The courts take the opportunity to construct quasi contracts when they find that the parties are in a type of relationship which involves obligations of some sort between them. For instance, through the construction of quasi contract, the courts have made parties who have caused harm by not taking action in a certain situation liable, where – if the relationship had been considered non-contractual – inactivity would not have given the injured person any legal right to compensation. Quasi contract is often considered to be at hand for shops, restaurants, etc. vis-à-vis people entering the premises, where the courts construct a contract-like obligation for the owner *vis-à-vis* visitors to protect them from harm.[32]

---

28. See NJA 1986 p. 712.
29. See NJA 2007 p. 758.
30. Chapter 35 s. 5 of the Code of Procedure.
31. See K. Grönfors, Avtalsgrundande rättsfakta, pp 98 et seq. (1993).
32. Compare NJA 1987 p. 692 and NJA 2001 p. 878. See also Part II Ch. 13.

§6. CONTRACT AND THE LAW OF PROPERTY

81. In Swedish Property Law (Sw: *sakrätt*) the distinction between right in personam (contract law) and right in rem (law of property) is no longer the only one used to distinguish property rights from obligatory rights. A right in personam means a right that is protected vis-à-vis a certain person, the contract party, whereas a right in rem is a right that is protected against everybody; in Swedish law this is expressed as a right protected against third persons. This type of right is also called a 'sakrätt', which refers to the fact that it has to do with an individualized object which is often – but not always – a 'thing' (Sw: *en sak*), i.e., property. In other jurisdictions the right in rem is called a 'real right' (droit reel). A right in rem can consist of a security right in the object in question which means that the person with the right does not own or even possess the object but has his claim against a debtor secured in the (value of) the object. Property law plays an important role especially in situations of insolvency, for instance in the case of bankruptcy, where several creditors compete for payment from the debtor.

82. Today, Swedish property law, does not rest solely on the distinction between rights in personam and rights in rem described briefly in §1 V above. To a larger extent the starting point is the question whether a right is protected against competing claims from third parties on the side of the creditor. Analysis of property law usually does not take its starting point in *rights* but in a *problem* which refers to all rights, i.e., to what extent ought certain rights to be protected from competing claims from third parties. The purpose of property law is seen to be to provide safe and good rules for ownership (the 'static' property law), and for transactions of property on the market (the 'dynamic' property law). With this approach there is no sharp and once and for all given distinction between rights in rem and rights in personam. Rights can be provided with a varying degree of protection against claims from third parties depending on the circumstances.

83. Under Swedish law there is no *numerus clausus* in property law in the sense that the number of recognized property rights is fixed. Quite another thing is that property rights that are not recognized by the law cannot be constituted by contract. Property law is mandatory in the sense that two parties to a contract do not have the right to determine that an obligatory right which they have created in their contract between the two of them should be respected by the rest of the world, i.e., enjoy legal protection against claims from third parties. Property law is mandatory for the protection of the interest of third parties.[33]

84. The most extensive right to property recognized by the legal system is the right which an owner has to the object he owns, he is then said to have title to the object (Sw: *äganderätt*). Ownership is seen as a bundle of rights – the most extensive – which the legal system at any given time grants a person as 'owner'. An owner is entitled to use, dispose of, etc his property to the extent that the legal system permits and this, at the same time, constitutes the definition of ownership. With

33. See however s. 54 of the Sales of Goods Act under Part II Ch. 4.

this way of looking at 'ownership', this position is not defined as something once and for all given, but, on the contrary, 'ownership' as a concept varies over time depending on the content of the legal system. The ownership of land or of a nuclear plant is much more restricted (by law) due to the public interest, due to risks, etc., than is, for example, the ownership of a bike.

85. Often, title to property passes from one person to another through contract. One cannot pass a more extensive title than one has. If transfer of property from A to B is agreed between A and B in a contract that turns out to be void, as a main rule, B cannot transfer the property to C, since B has not himself gained any title to the property in question. However, in Swedish law there is a special rule protecting receivers of movable property who are in good faith. Thus, if movable property (Sw: *lös sak*) which A does not own but which is in A:s possession, is transferred to B, for instance through a sales contract, B, if in good faith, receives title to the movable property once it comes into his possession. In order to prevent the transfer of movable property without title, for instance of goods belonging to someone else or of non-paid goods which one does not have the right to sell due to, for instance, a retention of title clause, with the help of this 'good faith protection' rule, the prerequisites for the good faith requirement have been made rather severe. Good faith can only be at hand if, judging from the type of goods in question, from the conditions under which they were offered and from the conditions in general, it seems likely that the receiver of the goods ought not to have suspected that the person transferring the goods did not have the right to transfer the title to them. This implies a duty for the buyer to investigate the ownership right of the seller in cases of transfer of goods which is often the subject of theft or of retention of title clauses or if the conditions around the sales transaction give reason for suspicion, for instance if valuable property is sold on an auction site on the internet. If good faith is not at hand, the real owner to the property has a right to recover it. In the case of stolen goods the owner retains the ownership even if the goods are transferred; here special rules for the protection of the owner apply.

86. A contractually based lien (Sw: *pant*), is an arrangement between a borrower and a lender through which the borrower designates his property as collateral for a loan from the lender. The deal involves two contracts, one regarding the lien and one regarding the loan. Such a lien must be registered with the authorities if the object is real estate or if it is movable property used in a business by a merchant (Sw: *företagshypotek*). For a lien in a specified object (chattel) to be valid, the object has to be transferred or taken out of the possession of the debtor. The lien is a property right interest in the sense that it gives priority for the creditor – to all other creditors – in the object subject to the lien if the borrower defaults on the loan. When the debtor defaults on his loan, the creditor who has a property right interest in the debtor's assets may demand seizure (Sw: *utmätning*) for his claim to foreclose on the property. The Enforcement Authority (Sw: *Kronofogdemyndigheten*) may then arrange for a compulsory auction without the debtor's consent. Obligatory duties with regard to the property, that the debtor might have taken upon himself through contract, may then have to yield for property rights, for instance a lien.

In this situation the strength of property rights over obligatory rights become evident. In NJA 2007 p. 455 a married couple who together co-owned a real estate had agreed in a written contract that it should not be permitted that the whole of the estate was sold in the Enforcement Authority procedure of compulsory auction but only the part owned by the party whose part was under seizure of the Enforcement Authority. Under the Act on Co-ownership (Sw: *lag 1904:48 om samäganderätt*) the main rule is that any one of the co-owners of property can demand the sale of the whole asset, unless the co-owners have agreed differently. A contract of the type just described had under the previous law been recognized as valid and, thus, prevented the compulsory sale of the whole estate demanded by a creditor with a lien against a debtor who only owned part of the real estate. In an *in pleno* decision the Supreme Court in NJA 2007 p. 455 changed the law and ruled that although the creditor only had a security interest right in half of the property (the wife's part), the contract between the parties should be disregarded and the whole estate could be sold under the compulsory auction procedure. Since selling just a part of a co-owned real estate does not attract many buyers (and, thus, would not be possible to sell at a good price) the Supreme Court held that the creditor's property right was stronger than the contract and implied that the whole estate should be sold and not just a part of it. The case is a good illustration of the competition between contractually based rights and property right interests and shows how property rights are rendered recognition at the expense of contractually based claims. The priority and the security provided by the law for property interests, for instance in the form of a lien, play an important role in the situation of bankruptcy where, usually, many creditors compete for payment from the debtor's assets.

I. No Distinction between Legal and Equitable Ownership

87. The distinction in Common law between legal and equitable ownership is not recognized in Sweden. There is nothing like the common law distinction between law and equity. Although ownership can imply different things for different types of property, there is only one form of ownership under Swedish law; either you are the owner or you are not. It is the property owner who has the right to take legal action against parties that attempt to infringe upon the ownership rights.

II. The Right of Usufruct

88. Usufruct is a concept that is not found in Swedish law. In jurisdictions where the concept exists, it means the right to use the property of another person and to enjoy the income from it without having to pay for the possession and use but only with a duty of care. Often, it seems to be an arrangement within a family sphere, mainly for the purpose of minimizing taxes. It is a right recognized as a right in rem, created through contract, for instance by sale or by gift, through will or by law. When usufruct is created the ownership is divided between 'bare ownership' and 'usufruct'. The usufruct ends with the death of the usufructuary at the latest (if the usufructuary is a legal entity in some jurisdictions the duration is thirty years) but it can also last for a shorter period of time. Usufruct should be registered with the authorities. There is nothing similar to this right in rem in Sweden. The closest one can find is the old concept of right to the yield (Sw: *avkastningsrätt*) which means a right established through contract, often together with the sale of real estate, providing a person – the seller – with a right to receive means for his support from the real estate in the form of money or *in natura*. Such a right could until 1972 be registered with the authorities and was then recognized as a right in rem in the sense that it was protected against a new owner of the property. Since such a right has been considered not to fill any practical purposes, it is no longer provided any property right protection.[34]

89. A tenant's lease of land (Sw: *arrende*) or of an apartment (Sw: *hyra av lägenhet*) is normally protected against a new owner of the real estate but a lease is not an a usufruct since the tenant or the leaseholder has to pay rent for his possession and use of the property.

III. Conveyancing

90. Ownership can be gained either in the form of a *derivative* acquisition, which means that one's right is derived from the earlier owner, for instance in the form of a sales transaction or a barter. In some rare cases, ownership can also be acquired through an *extinctive* acquisition meaning that the acquirer receives ownership in spite of the fact that he did not acquire the property from the right owner. His acquisition in this case extinguishes the right owner's title. Such can be the case if, in a sales transaction, chattel is sold by someone who has possession of the movable property without being the owner and the buyer is in good faith with regard to who has title to the goods. Finally, in very rare cases, ownership can occur by *originate* acquisition meaning that ownership originates with taking possession of a thing which has no owner, for instance things that have been thrown away. Such an acquisition is also called occupation. Things that have been lost and are found by somebody else do not belong to this category. Such findings should be notified to the police or – if the owner is known – to the owner. If the owner does not claim the found thing the finder may eventually become owner of the found item according to special regulation about lost and found things.

A. Agreement

91. As has become clear from the above, ownership can be transferred or acquired in various ways. The most common way to convey ownership and other property rights is through contract, through inheritance and will and, for a public body to acquire ownership, through expropriation. Most transfers of property rights are made through agreement, i.e., through contract, in the form of sale, gift or barter. In most cases, no special form is required and no notary or any other public

34. See H. Hessler, Allmän sakrätt, p. 314 (1973).

representative needs to be involved. Some transactions, however, require a certain form to be legally valid, for instance the transfer of real estate. Such a transaction requires written form and that certain information is included in the contract, such as the price, the identified property and the names of the seller and buyer. In the case of acquisition of real estate, the protection of the buyer's right against the claims of third parties increases by each step he has to take in the transaction and does not reach its full potential until the acquisition is registered with the authorities. Only certain types of conditions involving a pending ownership are permitted in the case of transfer of real estate.

B. Registration

92. Jurisdictions differ with regard to when a full property right is obtained, or, expressed differently, when property passes from one person to another. In some jurisdictions this happens at the time of the contract through which the parties agree to transfer the right, for instance in a sales contract. Sometimes the passing of property has to be intended by the parties of the contract to be valid. In other jurisdictions, to which Sweden belongs, the transfer of a right in rem is dependent on the transfer, the making public of or the registration of the object in question. Not until the buyer has received the object in his possession, has made his acquisition public or has had it properly registered – as is the case with real property – does he gain the full property right in terms of protection against claims from third parties. Once he has received such a protection for his property right he has priority to everybody else who claims any right to the same property.

93. Registration of acquisition of ownership is only required with regard to real estate. Sweden has a registration system of ownership of real estate which dates back several hundred years and which historically has played an important role as basis for taxation and the clarification of ownership of the Swedish territory. Today the system is completely electronically based.

§7. Contract and Trust

94. A trust under Common Law is a fiduciary relationship, created by a unilateral act and not through contract, usually as the result of a gift in which one person, the trustee, holds the legal title to property for the benefit of another, the beneficiary, or for charitable or other permitted purposes.

95. Trusts in the form known in Common Law are not recognized under Swedish law. The nearest equivalent form found is the foundation (Sw: *stiftelse*) which is an entity with legal personality, owned by itself – not a property ownership of anybody else – for the purpose of receiving property to be administered for and distributed to the beneficiaries of the foundation. A foundation is established when assets are set aside for the purpose of the foundation under the administration of a board of directors. A Swedish foundation, however, is not equivalent to the Common Law trust. The idea of equitable ownership does not exist in Swedish law which only recognizes the full ownership which – in turn – implies that the owner enjoys all rights provided for an owner by the legal system.

§8. Good Faith and Fair Dealing

I. Duty of Loyalty

96. Good faith and fair dealing is ubiquitous in Swedish contract law although it may not be recognized as a general principle as in e.g., German law. Considerations regarding good faith and fair dealing tend to blend with other policy considerations and are given more or less weight depending on the contractual context and the issue. In legal literature the requirement of good faith and fair dealing is generally referred to as a duty of loyalty. The exact meaning and scope of such duty is debated and legal doctrine is developing.

97. Good faith and fair dealing is closely related to the fundamental principle that the parties' reasonable reliance should be protected.

98. When a party accepts a duty of best efforts (*obligation de moyen*), the other party shall be able to rely on the first party's intention to loyally live up to the promise. When a party accepts a duty to achieve a specific result (*obligation de resultat*), the result must be as reasonably expected by the other party. A seller is consequently to deliver goods of a quality that meets the reasonable expectations of the buyer. A buyer shall be able to rely on the fact that the goods are suitable for his special purposes if the seller realized this purpose at the time of the contract and the buyer had due reason to rely on the seller's expertise; see section 17 of the Sale of Goods Act. This is tantamount to saying that the seller has a duty to prevent the frustration of the buyer's reasonable expectations. On the other hand however, a buyer may not invoke quality deficiencies if the seller has invited him to examine the goods, the buyer has failed to examine and he upon an examination could have discovered the deficiency. This caveat emptor rule is however set aside if the seller has acted dishonestly (Sw: *i strid med tro och heder*).[35]

99. It is a general principle that the party entitled to performance must cooperate so that the contract can be performed.[36]

100. Long-term contracts will typically give rise to ongoing loyalty obligations. Hence, a commercial agent is supposed to further the principal's interests and act in a loyal manner over the term of the agreement.[37] A duty of loyalty is also one of the essential ingredients for the employee in an employment contract.

---

35. See Sale of Goods Act s. 20.
36. See the Sale of Goods Act s. 48 para. 2 (seller's cooperation) and s. 50 (buyer's cooperation).
37. See Part II Ch. 1.

101. The duty of loyalty can be said to extend also to the exercise of remedies.[38] Above it was noted that the principal right to require specific performance could yield due to a balancing of the interest of the parties. This may be seen as a statutory expression of one aspect of a duty of loyalty. Likewise, the party entitled to performance may have to be active. Thus the right to require performance is lost if the entitled party waits for an unreasonably long time (since the inactivity can lead to the belief that the buyer has abandoned his claims).[39] There is also a notice requirement; the non-breaching party shall in frequent situations give notice of a breach to preserve his right present claims.[40] The moral underpinning of this notice requirement can be seen from the fact that the notice requirement does not apply if the party in breach has acted with gross negligence or been dishonest (Sw: *i strid med tro och heder*). Another outflow of an overreaching duty of loyalty is the burden of an injured party to mitigate his loss due to a breach of contract.

102. A reliance based duty of loyalty can also be seen in case law; passivity by one party has given rise to due reliance on the other side that an agreement has been met.[41] An agreement was considered to have been formed when a party received a written agreement ('Final Agreement') for signature after negotiations, but did not respond without undue delay. Here, upholding a 'duty of loyalty' can serve as behavioural instructions to parties in similar transactions.

103. A policy to uphold a duty of loyalty can be seen in some instances of contract interpretation where one party's omission to eliminate a misunderstanding on the other side can lead to an interpretation result that might otherwise have been different. This is usually referred to as the *dolus* model and *culpa* model for contract interpretation[42] for an illustration of the latter model.[43]

II. Duty of Cooperation

104. Supplementary rules may require cooperation between the parties. An example is section 50 of the Sale of Goods Act and CISG Article 60 which require the buyer to do the acts which could reasonably be expected of him in order to enable the seller to deliver the goods. It is submitted that a duty of reasonably expected co-operation is a term that a Swedish court would read into any contract as a supplementary rule based on reasonableness.

III. Inconsistent Behaviour

105. The policy to protect a party's reasonable reliance entails that a party cannot act inconsistently with an understanding that it has caused the other party to

38. Compare abuse of rights.
39. See the Sale of Goods Act s. 23 para. 3.
40. See e.g., the Sale of Goods Act s. 33.
41. See NJA 2006 p. 638.
42. See e.g., NJA 1951 p. 282 for an illustration of the former and NJA 1957 p. 69.
43. See also Adlercreutz & Gorton II, pp 132–137 (2010).

have, provided that the other party has relied on the understanding to his detriment. This principle can be seen as an outflow of the good faith and fair dealing tradition described above.

106. The understanding relied upon can be a result of a statement, of conduct or silence.[44] Typically the party who gives rise to an understanding is bound to it; the understanding becoming a part of the contractual relationship by means of contract interpretation.

107. The true meaning of this principle does however become clear only upon scrutiny of what kind of behaviour that the courts deem should give rise to justified reliance.

108. Statements regarding the quality of a party's own performance tend to be regarded as particularly worthy of reliance and they are typically treated as representations or warranties, the breach of which will lead to damage liability. The statements must however have a certain degree of precision, otherwise they will be regarded as unbinding puffery. A precise statement must also be made in close connection to the contract so that the receiving party can reasonably be deemed to have acted on it.[45] An incorrect response to buyer's question regarding a business' license to operate was not considered as a representation since it was given 'before … real contract negotiations begun'. [The seller was nevertheless responsible due to an omission to inform about limitations to the license, since he should have realized once the negotiations begun that the license was material to the buyer.] In between representations and puffery, there are statements that a party will be responsible for if he can be considered as negligent. The standard of negligence will typically be defined with consideration to the easiness to verify the accuracy of the statement and the foreseeable impact of the statement.

109. Affirmative conduct and even silence may equate a positive statement when the other party has cause to rely on the other party to avoid a misunderstanding.[46]

110. Behavioural aspects of the parties will in the situations pointed at above be considered in the interpretation process as facts in the preliminary negotiations (and be assessed against other interpretation data).

111. Inconsistent behaviour may also be of relevance during the course of a contract, either as interpretation data for the initial intention behind the agreement or as an acceptance of a subsequent contract modification (particularly in long-term agreements).

44. Compare NJA 2006 p. 638 (cited under I above).
45. Compare NJA 1991 p. 808.
46. Compare the Sale of Goods Act s. 17.

§9. STYLE OF DRAFTING

112. Swedish contracts are generally shorter than Anglo-American contracts. This is to some extent due to the absence of an equivalent to the Anglo-American parol evidence rule (excluding extrinsic evidence as regards the intentions of the parties). Nevertheless, in some areas of contract law draftsmen are influenced by the Anglo-American drafting style which leads to the use of whereas-clauses and the incorporation of boiler plate clauses. This can be seen particularly in contracts for mergers and acquisitions where the use of Anglo-American contract precedents is wide spread.

§10. SOURCES OF THE LAW OF CONTRACTS

113. There is actually no strict hierarchy of the sources of law but, nevertheless, with regard to how the law ought to be interpreted and applied, there is pretty much agreement among legal scholars, judges and practising lawyers how legal reasoning should be performed. The most important sources of law are the written statutes in the form of constitutional acts (Sw: *grundlagar*) and ordinary acts (Sw: *lagar*), i.e., the legislation enacted by the Swedish parliament. Even ordinances (Sw: *förordningar*) enacted by the government are considered authoritative sources of law. Since the legislative process is rather structured and formalized, the legislative history of the statute (*travaux préparatoires*) is considered an important source of law for the identification of the content of the statute with the pronouncement of the responsible minister and the report of the relevant standing committee of the Riksdag being the most important. The *travaux préparatoires* are often followed, but they are not formally binding. In addition – and this is where the Swedish legal system resembles the common law – precedents, i.e., decisions by the courts at the top of the court system (Supreme Court, Supreme Administrative Court, the Labour Court and the Market Court), although not formally binding, are also considered important sources of law in Sweden, more so than in other clear-cut civil law or code based systems. It is generally considered that precedents should be followed by the lower courts. In certain areas of private law, mercantile usages and customs play the role of sources of law.

114. The most important cases from the highest courts are published continuously on the internet and on a yearly basis in special publications. Decisions from the Supreme Court are published in 'NJA I' which is short for Nytt Juridiskt Arkiv (Eng: *New Legal Archive*). Reference to the cases is made in a standardized way indicating year and page.[47] The decisions from the Supreme Administrative Court are found in the publication 'HFD' which is short for Högsta förvaltningsdomstolen and are cited HFD 2014 ref. 15.[48] Until 2011 HFD appeared as 'RÅ' which stands

47. For example, NJA 2014 p. 15.
48. Indicating that the case is no. 15 in the publication.

for Regeringsrättens Årsbok. The reason for this is that The Supreme Administrative Court changed names from 'Regeringsrätten' to 'Högsta förvaltningsdomstolen' 2011. Cases from the Labour Court are found in the publication 'Arbetsdomstolens domar' (AD for short) and are referred to in the following way: AD 2014 nr 1. There is also a publication called NJA II which appears on a yearly basis. This publication contains the most important new statutes/amendments of statutes together with the most important legal preparatory works/legal history of these statutes.

115. Furthermore, there are various sources that may be taken into account, such as authoritative legal doctrine, and various forms of soft law instruments, such as recommendations and directives issued by public authorities or relevant private organizations.

I. The Norm Hierarchy

116. The sources of the law of contract can be structured along the following hierarchy:

(1) Mandatory rules;
(2) The agreement as interpreted intent;
(3) Practices which the parties have established between themselves;
(4) Custom and usage;
(5) Non-mandatory rules and judge made principles;
(6) Objective legal reasoning aiming at the creation of a supplementary gap-filling rule.

Items (1)-(4) and (5) are interrelated in a complex way.[49]

117. A few examples are given as an illustration. NJA 1970 p. 122 regarded a broker contract with exclusivity to sell a house during a fixed period of time. The principal (the house owner) revoked the broker's authority prematurely invoking the rules on revocation of the authority of agents. The Supreme Court found that the revocation amounted to a breach of contract with regard to the nature of the contract and what was established in similar contractual relationships. The court referred to the rules in the old Commission Agency Act (1914:45). NJA 1986 p. 503 regarded a provision in a lease contract which entitled the land lord to claim compensation for unforeseen costs. The question was whether he had the right to claim compensation for a new public fee imposed on house owners during 1982–1984. The Supreme Court found *inter alia* that a provision in Chapter 12 of the Land Code (1970:994), regulating lease contract, expressed the principle that rents should be

49. See A. Adlercreutz & L. Gorton, Avtalsrätt II, pp 13 et seq. (6 ed. 2010) [cit. Adlercreutz & Gorton II].

determined in advance, which according to the court supported a restrictive interpretation of the contract provision at dispute. Another case regarded a loan agreement including five co-sureties.[50] A clause gave the bank the right to reduce the security provided by the debtor without approval of the sureties. The bank released two of the co-sureties; the clause was interpreted restrictively due to the principle in the law on suretyship that the lender cannot reduce the liability of one co-surety which is bound *in solido* without the approval of the other co-sureties unless such right is specifically reserved. As regards item (2) and (5) preparatory works and legal literature will be influential for the legislative interpretation. As regards item (6) legal literature plays an important role. Likewise, international attempts to restate the law of contracts on a comparative basis, such as UNIDROIT Principles of International Commercial Contracts, Principles of European Contract Law and the Common Frame of Reference (DCFR) have come to be cited in support of judge made solutions.

II. Practices and Custom

118. Item (3) in the above norm hierarchy is to be further explained. When parties establish a practice among themselves, they are bound by it. Such practices may be established subsequent to a contract and amount to a modification of the contract.

119. Custom and usage (Sw: *handelsbruk och annan sedvänja*), i.e., norms that with a certain degree of firmness have been observed in an area of trade for a longer period due to a sense of obligation (*opinio juris*), prevail over non-mandatory rules[51] but yields to contract and practices. Custom is binding, provided that it is invoked and proved. Proof could earlier be submitted by the way of so-called *responsa*, i.e. investigations made by trade associations such as the Stockholm Chamber of Commerce but today the parties and the courts have to find other ways to clarify the existence of a custom.

50. NJA 1989 p. 269.
51. See Contract Act s. 1 para. 2, the Sales of Goods Act s. 3 and CISG Art. 9(2).

Part I. General Principles of the Law of Contract

Chapter 1. Formation

120. A contract may be concluded by the acceptance of an offer or by conduct of the parties provided that formal requirements have not been stipulated by any of the parties or follow by usages or practices or by statutory law. Contracts formed by the acceptance of an offer will be dealt with below.

121. Contracts may be formed by the conduct of the parties. The conduct must be such that the other party relies – or has due reason to believe – that the first party intends that the conduct shall be considered as a legal action.[52] A formal offer may be replaced by the act to make non-solicited goods or services readily available to the other party (de facto offer). A formal acceptance may be replaced by the act to pay or otherwise perform according to the offer or by the act to use or consume offered goods or services. The act to park a car on a parking lot with knowledge that payment is required is an example of an activity that constitutes a de facto acceptance of a de facto offer.

122. A formal acceptance can in certain circumstances also be replaced by an omission to act (passivity). Swedish law does in principle not recognize negative contracting. The recipient of non-ordered goods (a de facto offer) does not have to reject the goods in order not to be bound notwithstanding that the offeror may expect or even have stipulated that an omission to reject will be considered as an acceptance. The attempted use of negative contracting is considered as unfair marketing practice. A de facto offer of particular services, such as newspaper subscriptions or certain insurances, may however lead to a binding contract if the offeree fails to reject the offer. It is debated whether gratuitous offers and gifts will have to be accepted before the receiver is bound to receive the gift. The prevailing view seems to be that the receiver's passivity upon knowledge of the gift should be sufficient.[53] Formation of contracts due to passivity on the side of the offeree is known in commercial relations. Mere passivity is not sufficient. The passivity must have occurred in a context that gives rise to reliance on the side of the offeror that the passivity amounts to an acceptance. Such situations may foremost occur in ongoing

52. Compare UPICC Art. 2.1.1.
53. See Adlercreutz & Gorton I, p. 74.

business relations. In an established business relation between a principal and an commission agent (Sw: *kommissionär*), the agent must reject an offer to sell his services as an agent if he wishes not to be bound (3§ of the 2009 Commission Agency Act). In other agency contracts, a statutory rule (19§ Commercial Agency Act 1991: 351) requires that the principal rejects offers solicited by his agent if he wishes not to be bound (or the agent and the third party offeror have agreed that the offer shall lapse if not explicitly accepted by the principal). Passivity will be further dealt with in the section for the effects of late or modified acceptances below.

123. Formal requirements may be stipulated by one of the parties as a prerequisite for a binding contract. Formal requirements may also follow by usages or practices or by statutory law. Cases where a party has stipulated that a formal requirement (usually the signing of a written contract) shall be observed as a prerequisite for a binding contract needs to be distinguished from cases where the parties reduce their agreement into written form as a confirmation of what has already been agreed orally or agreed by other means. There is no definite default rule in Swedish law to apply in cases where it is unclear whether an understanding that a written contract shall be drawn up is to be regarded as a need for a confirmation or is to be regarded as a formal requirement. It is generally believed that the practical need to document the agreement in a contract shall be decisive. Thus the complexity, duration or value at stake may be important for the outcome.[54]

Formal requirements may also follow by statutory law.[55]

§1. Agreement and Quid Pro Quo (Reciprocity)

I. Offer and Acceptance

A. *Definition of Offer*

124. An offer is a legal act (Sw: *rättshandling*) and as such a declaration of a wish, will or intent to establish, change or terminate a legal relationship (Sw: *rättsförhållande*). Thus, an intent to establish a contract is an offer. This intent must be such that it is communicated to another party (the offeree) in an appreciable way. In reality, this means that the intent must be communicated in a way that is typically recognized in law. Therefore, an offer is an offer, with a certain legal effect, not due to the will as an independent phenomenon, but due to law. The legal principle is based on the policy in which purports that, what appears as an offer – in the sense that the offeree with due cause gets the impression that the offeror wants to establish a contract – is recognized as an offer. Yet, this policy yields in cases of illusory offers (i.e., offers made as a joke or otherwise without any serious intent). Such illusory offers are without legal effect *inter partes* even if the offeree relied on the offer.

54. See Adlercreutz I, p. 87.

55. Such is the case, for instance, regarding the transfer of real property.

An assignee of – what appears as – rights under an illusory agreement may however invoke the rights provided that the assignee did not know and had no due reason to suspect that the rights arose under an agreement that was devoid of legal effects.[56]

125. It is usually said that the consequence of when a legal act is recognized as an offer is that the offeror is bound by it.[57] This is an expression of the overreaching policy to protect the reliance of the offeree before the will of the offeror. The principle that an offer is binding has however many exceptions.

126. An offer becomes effective when it reaches the offeree. This has been accepted without any explicit provision in the Contracts Act, but is now confirmed in CISG Article 15(1). Thus, the transmission of an issued offer can be intercepted by the offeror before it reaches the offeree and the offeror can also withdraw the offer. Regarding withdrawal, see no. 132 below. Further modifications of the principle that offers are binding may follow from usage or practice. Yet, even if the 'offeror' declares that the 'offer' is not binding, he may nonetheless be bound by a response from an 'offeree' (typically in the form of an unmodified acceptance which is now regarded as a proper binding offer) if the 'offreror' must realize that the response is caused by the 'offer' and the 'offreror' does not reject the response without undue delay.[58]

127. An offer is usually made in the form of a statement but can also, due to the circumstances, be made by other conduct, e.g., the handing over of goods offered for sale. There are a number of general prerequisites for an offer (and other legal actions) to qualify for recognition under law beyond the now discussed imputed intent to establish a legal relationship.

128. First, the offer must be made by a person with legal capability or competence to conclude agreements. This means that duly created legal persons and natural persons above the age of 18 can make offers (with some exceptions for persons above the age of 16).

129. Second, the offer must be issued by the offeror.[59] This means that the offeror must have acted in such way that the action would typically lead to the effect that the offer is issued to the offeree.[60] In NJA 2000 p. 747 I, a seller signed a written contract under which it sold a piece of real estate to two buyers after which the buyers signed the contract and handed it to the real estate broker. Their acceptance was considered as issued by the handing over of the contract to a third party from whom the seller could have been informed about the acceptance. In NJA 2000 p. 747 II, the handing over of the contract to the signing party's own legal counsel did

56. See s. 34 of the Contracts Act.
57. See s. 1 para. 1 of the Contracts Act.
58. See s. 9 of the Contracts Act.
59. See s. 35 of the Contracts Act *e contrario*.
60. Compare NJA 2000 p. 747 I and II.

not amount to an acceptance. This rule was further elaborated in NJA 2012 p. 1095. Third, the offers must have one or more identifiable recipients.[61] An advertisement is not an offer, but is regarded as an invitation to make offers, unless the contrary is clear from the circumstances.[62] The receiver must be a natural or legal person. An offer cannot be made to e.g., an animal unless the animal is represented by a natural or legal person.

130. Fourth, the offer must be sufficiently precise[63] an agreement for the modification of commercial lease premises was considered not precise enough to give rise to an obligation to enter a subsequent lease agreement. The required precision varies with the type and function of the legal action and may be affected by the need to protect third party interests; the interest to avoid having to interpret the legal action in question in order to be able to ascertain his rights. Lacunae in an offer can be filled out by applicable non-mandatory default rules. E.g., an offer to sell goods without a quoted price will be filled out by the default rule that the buyer shall pay a fair price with regard to the goods, the prevailing price at the time of the contract and other circumstances at hand.[64]

131. Finally, it can be said that an offer must be received by the offeree in order for the offer to be given the effect of creating a contract. This means that the offeror can avoid any legal effects of the offer if he intercepts and prevents the transmission of an issued offer. This aspect does however not regard the definition of an offer *stricto sensu.*

B. Withdrawal of Offer

132. An offer can be withdrawn provided that the withdrawal reaches the offeree before or the same time as he takes part of the offer.[65] As regards withdrawal of an offer for the international sales of goods, CISG Article 15(2) applies, meaning that an offer, even if it is irrevocable, may be withdrawn if the withdrawal reaches the offeree before or at the same time as the offer. Thus, the possibility for an effective withdrawal is slightly wider under section 7 of the Contracts Act than under CISG Article 15 (2) – a difference that is offset by the possibility to revoke offers under CISG Article 16.

C. Revocation of Offer

133. Unless otherwise does not follow from the offer, custom or practice, an offer cannot be revoked during the stipulated time for acceptance or, lacking a

61. See CISG Art. 14(1).
62. See s. 9 of the Contracts Act and CISG Art. 14(2).
63. See NJA 1978 p. 147.
64. See s. 45 of the Sale of Goods Act. See also CISG Art. 14(1) and Art. 55.
65. See s. 7 of the Contracts Act.

stipulation, during a reasonable time period for acceptance. This is an expression of the promissory principle which is upheld in Nordic contract law, contrary to the contractual principle that in principle allows revocation of offers until acceptance; a principle upheld in common law.

134. The contractual principle is however to an extent upheld in regard to offers for international sale of goods according to CISG Article 16 with the significant modifications following from Article 16(2)(a) that an offer cannot be revoked during a stipulated time for acceptance or if it otherwise states that it is irrevocable and (b) that an offer cannot be revoked if it was reasonable for the offeree to rely on the offer as being irrevocable and the offeree has acted in reliance on the offer.

D. Rejection of Offer

135. If an offer is rejected, the effects of the offer terminates even if a stipulated period for acceptance has not come to an end.[66,67]

E. Mode of Acceptance

136. The acceptance is, like an offer, an example of a legal action and is subject to the same prerequisites as described in no. 124 above. An acceptance is a statement or other conduct that gives the offeror due reason to believe that the offer has been accepted. An acceptance can be inferred from an action such as the dispatch of goods as a response to an offer to buy or payment as a response to an offer to sell. Furthermore, the disposition over or consumption of goods sent to a buyer as an offer to sell is typically deemed to be an acceptance. This is now confirmed in CISG Article 18(3).[68] The act of parking a car on a parking lot was in principle held to be an acceptance of the conditions for parking, provided that the conditions are clear and readily available at the parking lot.

137. An acceptance becomes effective when it reaches the offeror.[69] In cases of acceptance by the performance of an action, the acceptance is most likely to be effective when the action cannot be stopped from coming to the offeror's knowledge. Under CISG Article 18(3), an acceptance by the performance of an action is effective when the action is performed.

138. In principle, silence or inactivity does not in itself amount to acceptance.[70] In some particular cases, inactivity is generally said to lead to the conclusion of a contract. This is true in regard to the renewal of newspaper subscriptions and

66. See s. 5 of the Contracts Act and CISG Art. 17.
67. See also s. 39 of the Contracts Act.
68. See NJA 1981 p. 323.
69. See CISG Art. 18(2). Compare s. 2 of the Contracts Act.
70. See CISG Art. 18(1).

renewal of certain insurances. Further exceptions to the principle that mere inactivity does not constitute an acceptance are seen when – foremost commercial relations – the parties have established a practice to perform without acceptance, in particular when the object of the contract can deteriorate with the passing of time or when the offeree would otherwise benefit from an option to speculate by remaining inactive. A commercial agent that is requested by an existing principal to perform services is further obligated to reject the request to avoid being bound. See section 3 of the Commission Agency Act and section 19 of the Commercial Agency Act. Swedish judicature contains some examples of a similar effect of inactivity on part of the offeree with the aim to protect the offeror's justified reliance that preliminaries to an agreement have been accepted.[71] An offeree was deemed to have caused the offer (in the form of a signed standard agreement) and must have understood that the offeror assumed that the standard agreement was accepted unless the offeree rejected within a reasonable time.[72]

F. Time of Acceptance

139. An acceptance is not effective if it does not reach the offeror within the time stipulated by him or, if no time has been stipulated, within a reasonable time limit. What is a reasonable time is determined with due regard to the circumstances, including the time an offeree (who may be a commercial actor or a consumer) might need to consider the offer and the rapidity of the means of communication employed by the offeror. An oral offer must be accepted immediately, unless the circumstances indicate otherwise.[73]

140. An offeror – who according to the Contracts Act in principle is bound to stand by his offer – can eliminate doubts as to whether the time for an acceptance is still running by asking whether the offeree accepts (Sw: *interpellation*). If the offeree fails to respond, the offer is ineffective.[74]

G. Late Acceptance

141. An acceptance which does not reach the offeror within the time stipulated by him or, if no time has been stipulated, within a reasonable time is not effective as an acceptance and the offeror is no longer bound by his offer. The late acceptance is deemed to be a new offer according to which the issuer of the late acceptance is bound.[75]

---

71. See NJA 1962 p. 276.
72. See also NJA 2006 p. 638 also indicating a room for analogous application of s. 19 of the Commercial Agency Act.
73. See ss 2 and 3 of the Contracts Act and CISG Art. 18(2).
74. See s. 8 of the Contracts Act.
75. See s. 4 para. 1 of the Contracts Act.

142. In regard to the international sale of goods, a similar principle applies under CISG Article 21. Here, an offeror can chose to regard a late acceptance as being timely by informing the offeree, without undue delay, that the acceptance shall be considered as effective. The consequence is then that an agreement is formed as of the point of time when the late acceptance reached the offeror.

H. Delay in Transmission of Acceptance

143. There is an exception to the main principle in that a late acceptance is essentially ineffective. According to section 4 paragraph 2 of the Contracts Act, a late acceptance leads to a contract, if the offeree in good faith believes that the acceptance has reached the offeror in time and the offeror must have realized the offeree's belief and nevertheless does not give notice to the offeree that the acceptance was late and that the offeror rejects it. See also CISG Article 21(2) with its objective test:

> If a … writing containing an acceptance shows that it has been sent in such circumstances that if its transmission had been normal it would have reached the offeror in due time.

144. The subjective test under section 4 paragraph 2 of the Contracts Act and the objective test under CISG Article 21(2) will most likely not have any practical significance, although the realm of circumstances that could be considered by the court appears to be wither under the Contracts Act. A typical example of a situation when a delayed acceptance can lead to a contract due to passivity on the side of the offeror is when the dating and mail stamp of the acceptance shows that the offeree had reason to believe that the acceptance reached the offeror in time. It is believed that this rule can be applied by analogy in cases where the acceptance is lost in the transmission.

I. Withdrawal of Acceptance

145. An acceptance can be withdrawn based on the same principles that apply to a withdrawal of an offer pursuant to section 7 of the Contracts Act.[76]

J. Modified Acceptance

146. A reply to an offer which purports to be an acceptance but contains additions, limitations or modifications is regarded as a rejection of the offer and is treated as a counter-offer pursuant to section 6 paragraph 1 of the Contracts Act and CISG Article 19(1).

---

76. See s. 2.3 above.

147. An exception to the main rule is expressed in section 6 paragraph 2 of the Contracts Act. A modified acceptance can lead to a contract, if the offeree in good faith believes that the acceptance corresponds to the offer, the offeror must realize the offeree's belief and the offeror notwithstanding this does not without undue delay gives notice to the offeree that the acceptance shall be deemed to be a modified acceptance.[77] Again, the Contracts Act, in the same way as in the case of delayed acceptance, builds on a subjective test, which has been abandoned in CISG Article 19(2). Here modifications which do not materially alter the offer require the offeror to be active unless he shall be bound by the modified acceptance. The provision in Article 19(2) is to be read together with Article 19(3) which enumerated kinds of modifications whom are substantial per se and which consequently require no activity on the side of the offeror. As in the case of section 4 of the Contracts Act, it may be assumed that the subjective versus the objective test in the CISG will have a limited practical importance.

K. Writings in Confirmation

148. The provisions on modified acceptance are related to the principles that apply when a message that purports to be a confirmation is sent to a party in conjunction with the conclusion of a contract. If such message contains additional or different terms than those which appear in the offer and acceptance, the question arises whether the receiver of the message is bound by its contents. This would have particular practical importance when the contract has been formed orally, and the conclusion of the contract is followed by a 'confirming' message in writing with a view to create evidence as regards the contents of the contract. It should be noted that in cases where one of the parties have reserved the right to 'confirm' the contract, the 'confirmation' is to be regarded as an acceptance in a technical sense. If however, one of the parties has conditioned the binding effect of an offer or acceptance on the fulfilment of an objective condition (such as the grant of an export license), a message that the condition has been fulfilled would be deemed to be a confirmation rather than an acceptance.

149. A confirmation should serve as evidence. The evidentiary value of a one sided confirmation as such is not particularly strong since it reflects only one party's understanding. Passivity on the side of the receiver will nevertheless increase the evidentiary value.

150. There is no generally applicable statutory rule to this effect. The evidentiary value attributed to passivity appears to vary with the circumstances and context.[78]

77. Compare NJA 2006 p. 638.
78. Compare NJA 1977 p. 25 below.

151. Section 21 of the Commercial Agency Act can be applied by analogy in commercial contracts: A party who has negotiated with an agent regarding a commercial contract and who receives a confirmation from the agent's principal must give a notice of rejection unless he shall be bound or show that the 'confirmation' incorrectly restates the agreement made or that an agreement was never made. Thus, the provision expresses a presumption for the accuracy of the confirmation unless the receiver objects without undue delay. The principle under section 21 of the Commercial Agency Act was analogously applied in NJA 2006 p. 638 (a party received a document called final agreement for signing but did not reject the document without undue delay and was consequently bound by the contents of the document).

152. Another avenue to resolve problematic cases opens by an analogous application of section 6 paragraph 2 and section 9 of the Contracts Act.

153. NJA 1977 p. 25 regarded an order for certain hospital equipment made by a district medical. The seller (a foundation) sent an order confirmation which was not rejected by the hospital. The Supreme Court did not apply the principle under section 6 paragraph 2 and section 9 of the Contracts Act nor the principle under section 21 of the Agency Act, holding that the nature and scope of the relations between the parties was not such that the passivity on the side of the hospital should lead to the conclusion of a contract irrespective of what the seller had meant by its order confirmation and what the hospital might have understood of the seller's intentions.

154. A confirmation with or without passivity on the side of the receiver may also be of importance in the process of interpreting a contract.[79]

L. Notices

155. Notices include declarations of intent, requests and claims. A notice shall generally be sent by appropriate means (Sw: *på ett försvarligt sätt*).

156. A notice in the process of contract formation is sent on the receiver's risk, if a failure to give notice would result in the conclusion of an agreement, the acceptance of an offer or a legal action is binding. This sets a limitation to the protection of a party who in good faith believes that a contract has been formed or that the other party has become bound by a legal action. A notice withdrawing the authority of an agent shall be given in the same manner as the authority of the agent was communicated.[80]

157. A buyer's request for performance, a notice that termination will be made due to a delay notwithstanding delivery, notice that buyer reserves the right to claim damages due to delay, notice of non-conformity of the goods, request for remedial

79. See Adlercreutz & Gorton I, pp 85 et seq.
80. See Contracts Act s. 40.

action, notice of termination, rejection of invoiced price and a notice of inhibition of performance due to anticipated breach are all sent on the seller's risk. Correspondingly, a seller's notice of a requirement for continued performance, a request for buyer's cooperation of delivery, a notice of termination or a damage claim due to breach and notice of inhibition of performance due to anticipated breach are sent on the buyer's risk.

158. These provisions are generally believed to apply by analogy expressing the policy that the party in whose interest the notice is sent shall carry the risk that the notice does not reach him.

159. A notice is considered to have reached the receiver when it is delivered at that party's mailing address. The fact that the receiver has not read or otherwise taken part of it is irrelevant. However, when the effect of a legal act (e.g., an offer) depends on whether the receiver was ignorant of a circumstance voiding the legal act (e.g., a subsequent notice withdrawing the offer), the knowledge at the time when the legal act became actually known to him is decisive. Under special circumstances (such as abuse of rights) later knowledge may also be considered and relieve the acting party from the consequences of this action. Contracts Act section 39 (the so-called *re integra* rule).

M. Conclusion of Contracts Dependent on Agreement on Specific Matter or in a Particular Form

160. Swedish law adheres to the principle that a contract is concluded if the parties reach agreement on the essential terms, while minor terms are left open to be subsequently resolved or be settled by gap-filling mandatory rules or practices. This principle is however not applied in cases where a party makes it clear that the contract shall not come into existence without agreement on the terms left open. The same applies when a party makes clear that the agreement must be reduced to writing or any other form before it becomes binding (to be distinguished from cases where the contract is mutually confirmed by a written document). The problem here is in determining how clear or express the party who does not wish to be bound must be. In regards to a requirement for a written contract, the line between a confirmation effect and a prerequisite for the conclusion of the contract seems to be drawn depending on the practical need to draw up a written contract.[81]

N. Contracts with a Term Deliberately Left Open

161. A contract must have a certain degree of definiteness. Hence, the parties cannot deliberately leave essential terms open unless there is a gap-filling mechanism provided by practice or law. Apart from this remark, the principle is that

81. See Adlercreutz & Gorton I, pp 93 et seq.

a contract with terms deliberately left open will be effective. Hence, the incompleteness cannot be invoked as a ground for invalidity when the parties have been aware of the incompleteness. This case is to be distinguished from cases where only one party has been aware of the incompleteness. Mutual awareness may be inferred from the circumstances, such as the non-essential character of the gaps and the difficulty to close the gaps at the time of the contract.[82]

O. Letters of Intent

162. A document that is in principle not binding is often referred to as a letter of intent. The extent to which letters of intent can lead to legal effects is debated.

163. NJA 1992 p. 375 regarded a letter of intent issued by a municipality regarding financial support to one of its companies in favour of a bank. The bank argued that the document in effect amounted to a financial guarantee. The Supreme Court noted that a guarantee would have required the formality of approval by a municipality meeting, but that this did not exclude the possibility that the municipality could be liable for damages due to incorrect information or withholding new information from the bank. The bank was however considered to be equally involved in the company's project and that it knew as much of the project as the representatives of the municipality.

164. Furthermore, NJA 1994 p. 204 regarded a letter of intent issued by a parent company stating that the parent company intended to financially support its subsidiary if needed in the future. The letter was issued to a supplier of steel. The letter was considered to be a prerequisite for its willingness to deliver the steel to the subsidiary. The parent company allowed its subsidiary to file for bankruptcy and was held liable to compensate the suppliers' losses.[83]

P. Merger Clauses and Clauses on Modification in a Particular Form

165. A clause stating that a written contract completely embodies the terms on which the parties have agreed is usually referred to as a merger clause or an integration clause. Such clauses are generally used with a view to emphasize the importance of the written terms, but are presumably not enough to set aside the principle of free evaluation of presented evidence which is upheld in Swedish procedural law. The effect of a merger clause is therefore believed to further increase the evidentiary value of the written contract as a record of what the parties really have agreed. A merger clause will therefore not limit the relevance of prior statements and practice in the process of interpreting unclear agreements.[84]

82. See J. Ramberg, Medveten otydlighet som avtalsrättsligt problem, JT 1992/93 p. 358.
83. Compare NJA 1995 p. 586.
84. Compare UPICC Art. 2.1.17.

166. It is also common that parties, particularly in commercial contracts, insert a clause stating that the agreement may not be amended or changed unless made in writing (signed by both parties). Such clauses (no oral amendment clauses) will not preclude a party from relying on the other party's conduct as a de facto acceptance of a contract modification. In the area of international sales of goods, this follows directly from CISG Article 29(2).[85]

Q. Contracting under Standard Terms

167. Where one or more parties use standard terms in the process of concluding a contract, the latter rules on contract formation apply. Standard conditions can be attached or referred to in an offer or attached to or referred to in an acceptance – which would usually mean that the acceptance is regarded as a modified acceptance. When parties use standard conditions, they would usually negotiate and agree on the material terms such as what, when and how much each party is expected to perform ('dickered terms'). The rest of the agreement follows from the standard conditions. Standard conditions may be drawn up by one of the parties unilaterally. Such standard conditions can serve as a starting point for negotiations or be of a 'take-it-or-leave-it' character. Standard conditions can also be produced by a branch organization and be more or less one sided, or result from negotiations between branch organizations representing both parties' interests ('agreed documents'). Such agreed documents may to some extent serve as evidence of usages and practices and be given a gap-filling function akin to non-mandatory statutory provisions. Examples of such Swedish agreed documents are AB 04 and ABT 06 for building, construction and installation services. Examples of Nordic agreed documents are the widely used NL 09 – for deliveries of mechanic, electric or electronic equipment within and between the Nordic countries and NLM 10 which includes erections services, acceptance tests and rights to software in the deliverables. These agreements are drawn up in cooperation between Nordic organizations representing the technological industry and purports to represent both vendor and purchaser interests.

168. The use of one sided standard conditions in commercial transactions can be restricted under the Act (1984:292) on Commercial Contract Terms; the Market Court can prohibit the future use of unreasonable standard terms if it is warranted from a public interest point of view. The act has rarely been used. See however MD 2010:12; in which a clause restricting competition was not prohibited. Unreasonable standard terms as well as unreasonable individually negotiated terms may be adjusted or set aside as unreasonable under section 36 of the Contracts Act.

85. Compare UPICC Art. 2.1.18. See L. Gorton, The Nordic Tradition: application of boilerplate clauses under Swedish law, pp 276 et seq. in Cordero-Moss, G. [ed.], Boilerplate Clauses, International Commercial Contracts and the Applicable Law – Common Law Contract Models and Commercial Transactions Subject to Civilian Governing Laws (2011).

169. As for standard conditions and other non-negotiated terms in consumer contracts the flexibility in the application of section 36 has been limited under section 11 of the Act (1979:417) on Consumer Contract Conditions, which was introduced in the process of implementing the Council Directive 93/13/EEC of 5 April 1993 on unfair terms in consumer contracts. Thus, subsequent events that would otherwise have led to the conclusion that a contract term is not unreasonable pursuant to section 36 shall be disregarded. If the consumer requests that an unreasonable term shall be set aside and the rest of the contract shall remain without adjustment, the consumer's request shall be granted. There is no counterpart to section 11 of the Act on Consumer Contract Conditions that applies to commercial contract and consequently the flexibility in the application of section 36 remains in this area.

170. The possibility to use section 36 to adjust or set aside unreasonable contract terms even in commercial contracts means that there is no need in Swedish law to adhere to such principles as expressed in e.g., UPICC Article 2.1.20 stating that surprising standard terms are ineffective unless expressly accepted. However, the fact that a term is surprising by virtue of its content *may* lead to adjustment under section 36 if it is clear that the other party hardly would have accepted the term if he had been aware of it. Equally, a term may be adjusted or set aside if it has been presented so as to avoid the attention of the other party, e.g., in minute print or by being imbedded in other clauses. Obscure terms would however primarily be subject to interpretation.[86]

R. Conflict between Standard Terms and Non-standard Terms

171. Another matter relating to interpretation of standard terms regard conflicts between standard terms and non-standard terms. The situation may be that an individually agreed term may conflict with the standard terms. In such cases the rule is that the individually agreed terms prevail over the standard terms.[87]

S. Battle of Forms

172. Where both parties use standard terms the rules on modified acceptance come into play. If the two set of terms are materially different, the modified acceptance would be considered as a rejection in combination with a new offer.[88] The situation may however be problematic if the first offeror is excused from not having noted that the offeree referred to its terms in the modified acceptance. The outcome of a battle of forms, i.e., cases where both parties start to implement the agreement (or none of them claims that the agreement shall be declared ineffective) in awareness of the fact that they have referred to conflicting standard terms is not settled in

86. See *infra*.
87. Compare UPICC Art. 2.1.21. See Adlercreutz & Gorton II, p. 61.
88. Se no. 146 *supra*.

Swedish law. The principle set forth in UPICC 2.1.22 does not resolve what the agreement shall be deemed to be on issues where the terms are incompatible, e.g., the case that the seller's terms allows for price revision and the buyer's terms state that the price is fixed.

173. In legal literature, the general view is that the matter should not be settled by an attempt to mechanically apply section 6 of the Contracts Act. A pragmatic approach is generally advocated. One view is that the terms proposed by the party who shall render specific performance shall prevail, at least when the terms have had an impact on the offered price. Another view is that the terms that are most akin to the terms frequently used in transactions of the kind in question shall prevail. A third solution is to let the conflicting terms neutralize each other and apply gap-filling practices or non-mandatory rules as far as such rules are available. All these approaches can most likely be amalgamated into the view that a term that best corresponds to the nature and purpose of the transaction shall apply as far as the interests of foreseeability allows.[89]

II. Intention to Create Legal Relations

174. The requirement in English law, where a promise, in order to be legally enforceable, must be followed by consideration from the promisee or included in a deed from the promisor properly executed, does not exist in Swedish law. Under English law, a party who intends to be bound, but who does not make his promise either in a deed or in return for consideration, is not legally bound, and this has in turn created a doctrine in English law of 'intention to create legal relations'.[90] In Sweden, there is no distinction between 'intention to be bound' and 'intention to create legal relations'.

175. Under Swedish law, in order for a promise to be legally relevant as an offer, the offeror must have an intention to become legally bound/to create legal relations. This is expressed by classifying such a promise a 'juridical act' (Sw: *rättshandling*). In the legal history of the Contracts Act, dating back to 1915, the concept 'juridical act' is said to imply 'any expression of will which have as its purpose to establish, alter or terminate a legal relationship' (Sw: *alla viljeförklaringar, vilka hava till syfte att grundlägga, förändra eller upphäva ett rättsförhållande*), This old text expresses the view from that time where the will as the constituting element of a contract is emphasized. Today, although the will of the parties is, of course, still an important element in the formation of an enforceable contract, the will of a party (to be bound) is conceived more objectively, i.e., in the way which it could reasonably be expected to be understood by the other party. Today, the meaning of a 'rättshandling' in Swedish law seems to correspond, in general, with the definition of a

89. See Adlercreutz & Gorton II, pp 85 et seq. and U. Göransson, Kolliderande standardavtal (1988).
90. See Cartwright, 2007, p. 140.

juridical act found in the Draft Common Frame of Reference, Chapter 1, II.-I:I0I(2):

A juridical act is any statement or agreement or declaration of intention, whether express or implied from conduct, which has or is intended to have legal effect as such. It may be unilateral, bilateral or multilateral.

176. Under Swedish law, it is sometimes emphasized that a contact actually consists of two juridical acts, i.e., two 'rättshandlingar', offer and acceptance, which correspond to each other.

177. A party who gives a promise in the form of a juridical act, i.e., with the intention to be legally bound, is bound by that promise during a period of time referred to as the 'acceptance period'. If the acceptance from the offeree comes to him before the acceptance period has elapsed, and the acceptance is clear, i.e., corresponds to the offer, then there is a contract. Normally, no other formalities, no consideration nor anything else is required.

178. If a party tries to challenge a contract with the argument that he did not have an intent to be bound, he has the burden of proof to establish that there is no binding contract.[91]

III. Consideration

A. The Common Law Doctrine of Consideration

179. There is no equivalent in Swedish law to the common law consideration doctrine.[92]

B. Gratuitous Promises

180. Since old times, a gift of personal property (Sw. *lös egendom*) requires a promise in a document which is handed over to the receiver, a public promise or the handing over of the given object. Section 1 of the Act on Gifts (1936:83). The same holds for loans of personal property and interest free credits. In some cases, registration is required.[93] A gift of a negotiable debt instrument requires the handing over of the instrument. A gift of a non-negotiable debt note is however effective when the receiver obtains knowledge about the gift.[94]

---

91. See, for instance, the judgment of Hovrätten för Västra Sverige, 2008-03-19, case nr 2863-07.
92. Compare however 1.1 §1 III.B below.
93. See ss 2–3 of the Act.
94. See s. 3 of the Act. See J. Hellner, R. Hager, & A. Persson, Speciell avtalsrätt II, 1 st binder, pp 270 et seq. (5th ed. 2010) [cit. Hellner II:1.].

§2. FORMAL AND EVIDENTIAL REQUIREMENTS

I. Formal Requirements

181. The main principle establishes that oral agreements are binding (although obviously harder to prove). This is explicitly set forth in CISG Article 11 and follows indirectly from section 1 paragraph 3 of the Contracts Act. Hence, there is no requirement for e.g., consideration.[95]

182. Traditionally, contracts for the sale of real estate have been required to be in written form. These requirements have been turned into statutory writing requirements for the majority of real estate transactions (furthering a public interest to induce thoughtfulness, secure evidence and transparency for affected third parties). See e.g., as for the sale of land (Chapter 4 section 1 of the Land Code) and for land lease contracts (Chapter 8 section 3 of the Land Code). Form requirements do not exclude the possibility to have regard to extrinsic facts in the interpretation of the agreement.[96]

183. A writing requirement is upheld in respect to real estate broker contracts with the object to protect a typically weaker non-professional party. This interest is generally the motive for upholding various form requirements in consumer contract law; e.g., consumer credit contracts and in distance selling contracts (with information and confirmation requirements). The lack of form will generally not operate to the detriment of the consumer.

184. Form requirements are also seen in labour law; collective bargaining agreements require written form.

185. Form requirements should be distinguished from requirements in regard to documentation that is part of the obligations of one of the parties; e.g., the obligation of the employer to subsequently inform about the terms and conditions for the employment.

186. Contractual form requirements include a statutory duty to formalize in writing e.g., lease contracts (Chapter 12 section 2 of the Land Code) and commercial agency agreements upon request by a party. This is not a form requirement *stricto sensu*; a refusal to formalize the contract in writing is a breach and may have evidentiary repercussions.

187. The parties may also agree that they shall not be bound until the signing of a written agreement. This is often combined with a provision that the agreement may not be modified orally and that modifications shall be made in writing. This is common in commercial contracts. Such clauses are however deemed not to preclude a party from showing that a binding oral agreement has nevertheless been

95. See however s. 1.III.B above.
96. See e.g., NJA 1955 p. 247 and NJA 1984 p. 482.

formed, although the requirements on the evidence in support of such agreement is so high that the possibility is open only in exceptional cases.

A. *Contracts under Seal*

188. There are no contracts under seal in Swedish law.

B. *'Solemn' Contracts*

189. The concept of 'solemn' contracts is not used in Swedish law. The form requirement on contract for the sale of real estate may functionally correspond to the concept.[97]

II. Evidential Requirement: Proof

A. *The Parol Evidence Rule*

190. There is no equivalent to the Anglo-American parol evidence rule in Swedish law.[98]

B. *No Notary*

191. There is no notary function in Swedish contract law. Documents which have to be recorded by the court's registrar system such as ante-nuptial agreements (Sw: *äktenskapsförord*), mortgages and the transfer of real property, do not have to be prepared by a notary. The role of the notary function in Sweden is only to acknowledge the formalities of documents, for instance to acknowledge that a translation of a document is accurate.

III. Burden of Proof

A. *General Observations on Burden of Proof*

192. As a starting point, the burden of proof, according to the traditional dogmatic school, rests upon the party who asserts a legally relevant circumstance. Deviations from the general rule are often motivated when the other party has had

97. See no. 182 above. Compare also 1.1 s. 1 III.B above.
98. See further no. 304.

the better opportunity to secure evidence. The burden of proof may also be shifted in cases when this is considered motivated in order to promote policies that underpin the legal rule in question.

193. In regard to contracts it can be said that the party who asserts that a contract has been made has the burden of proof. When a contract is proven, its contents is to be presumed to correspond to the prima facie understanding of wording. In respect to the price, the main rule is that in sales contracts or contracts for work, the party who asserts that a fixed price has been agreed or asserts a particular mechanism for determining the price has the burden of proof.[99]

B. Obligation of Means and Obligation of Result

194. In modern Swedish legal literature it is not common practice to build on the distinction between obligations to achieve a specific result (*obligations de résultat* or Sw: *resultatförpliktelser*) versus best effort obligations to try achieving a specific result or the best possible result (*obligations de moyen* or Sw: *omsorgsförpliktelser*).[100] Rather, obligations of specific performance are often divided along the remedy related criteria of time (delay) and quality (defects).[101]

195. Payment obligations (which are regarded as obligations to achieve a specific result) are often dealt with separately. The method can lead to systematical difficulties when it comes to central best effort obligations such as the obligation of the commercial agent to diligently strive to maximize the sales of the principal's goods and in other respects further his interests. Such systematical problems seem to concern scholars more than practitioners and judges and it is self-evident that a party who is deemed to be obliged to abide by a best effort standard has to make such efforts as would be made by a reasonable person of the same kind in the same circumstances. The implication of the latter is closely interrelated to the definition of negligence (*culpa*). The non-occurrence of a promised result amounts to non-performance regardless of any negligence when the obligor is under a duty to achieve a specific result, such as the delivery of goods at a certain place on a certain time. The consequences follow from the remedies available to the obligee. When the obligor is under a duty of best efforts, non-performance occurs as soon as the best effort standard is not observed by the obligor. The standard of best effort can briefly be described as the lack of negligence. Again, the consequences if a duty of best efforts is set aside are defined by the remedies that are available to the obligee. The available remedies may vary between different types of contracts and may also depend on the germaneness of the obligation set aside.

---

99. See NJA 1989 p. 215 and NJA 2001 p. 177.
100. See however K. Rodhe, Obligationsrätt, pp 20 et seq.
101. See Hellner et al., II, 2nd binder, p. 32 (2010) [cit. Hellner II:2].

§3. LIABILITY AND NEGOTIATIONS

196. Liability for acts and omissions during contract negotiations tend to regard behaviour that casts doubt upon the assumption that both parties have acted with free will. Typically, this leads to the question whether the contract should be declared null and void. This is the case where the contract is made under threat or is caused by fraud or usury. Another type of situation encompasses the question of whether the fact that one party has withheld information that was of relevance for the other party's decision to enter into the contract. This regards the question of whether the other party has reason to rely on the other party to divulge the information in question. An omission to inform could lead to invalidity due to fraud. It is also possible that invalidity may result under any of the general clauses in the Contracts Act sections 33 or 36 or pursuant to the doctrine of failed assumptions.[102] It is however also possible that the contract stands although the first party is liable for quality deficiencies in its performance. See e.g., the Sale of Goods Act section 17 paragraph 2 point 2: the goods must conform to the buyer's specific purpose if the seller ought to have known this purpose and the buyer had reason to rely on the seller's expertise and judgment. See also section 19: even if the goods are sold 'as is', the goods are considered defective if the seller omitted to inform the buyer about substantive features of the goods that he was aware of and the buyer could reasonably expect to be informed about provided that such information can be deemed to have influenced the purchase. In a general sense, all these situations encompass negotiations in bad faith (*culpa in contrahendo*). In a more narrow sense, negotiations in bad faith refer to situations where one party negotiates without any real intention to ultimately form a contract or otherwise is to blame for the non-occurrence of a contract. These situations regard behavioural aspects of the negotiation process and they may give rise to questions regarding precontractual liability.

I. Precontractual Liability

197. The doctrine of precontractual liability in Swedish law limits the freedom of contract during the precontractual phase. Precontractual liability relates to the parties' conduct during the contractual negotiations. It puts on the parties a duty of loyalty, i.e., a duty to deal in good faith with each other during the negotiations and during the formation of the contract. The precontractual liability rules are not there to protect a party's interest to reach an agreement, rather to protect a party's interest in not having to suffer economic loss or other injuries during the bargaining process. The purpose is to protect the 'reasonable reliance' on a promise (Sw: *den faktiska tillitens relevans*) and to do this by awarding damages for reasonable expenditures incurred as a result of this reliance (when no contract has come about). However, a party has to be found substantially negligent in order to have to pay damages to the other party for his conduct during the precontractual phase; the overriding principle still being the freedom of contract with the right for each party to withdraw without any particular reason.

102. See Introduction s. 1 III.

198. There is no explicit regulation in the Contracts Act or elsewhere regarding precontractual liability. The doctrine has developed through case law.[103] A recent case is the Swedish Supreme Court is NJA 2012 p. 1095 where the Supreme Court – obiter dictum – discusses the legal consequences in terms of possible damages when a party, during negotiations regarding the transfer of real property, acts without due consideration of the other party's interest. The possibility to award damages in such a situation is said by the Court to be preferred in front of extending the scope of the contract 'mechanism' regulating the transfer of real property.

A. *Breakdown of Negotiations*

199. The issue of precontractual liability is about liability in situations where no contract has been concluded between the negotiating parties. If a contract is actually concluded, a party's conduct during the negotiations is usually dealt with within the contractual sphere, i.e., as a matter of contractually based obligations.

200. As a general statement, it is most accurate to say that the Swedish doctrine of precontractual liability is a form of delictual/tortious liability based on a general principle of loyalty, i.e., a liability that is not contractually based. However, one also finds the opinion amongst scholars that the liability is neither contractually nor delictually based but that, instead, it should be seen as a special form of liability, a *tertium quid* between contract and tort, based directly on the relationship between the negotiating parties which is not a contract, nor a relationship between strangers, as in tort.

201. Whether in Swedish law precontractual liability should be seen as resting on a general principle of loyalty, i.e., delictually/tort based, or contractually based, might not be as important to determine. This is because the courts appear to put much emphasis on the circumstances in the particular case when making a determination and since under the doctrine of precontractual liability the damages never amount to more than damages for the reliance interest. There is no doubt, however, that the Swedish courts see the relationship between the parties during the precontractual phase as a relationship which in one way or the other deserves the protection of the law, but, at the same time, they are reluctant to award compensation for costs incurred during this phase.

202. According to Swedish law, initially, during contract negotiations, the good faith requirement merely implies that a party has to act honestly and decently and observe reasonable commercial standards of fair dealing between merchants of the trade/profession in question. However, the further the negotiations proceed, the more the parties are obliged to act loyally, i.e., to also consider the interest of the other party. At a later stage in the contract negotiations where the parties appear

103. In Sweden the most frequently cited Supreme Court cases are NJA 1963 p. 105, NJA 1973 p. 175, NJA 1978 p. 147 and NJA 1990 p. 745. See e.g., Adlercreutz & Gorton I, pp 119 et seq.

close to the conclusion of the contract it might be considered negligent to one-sidedly withdraw from the negotiations without a legitimate cause. Liability for such conduct can occur in the situation where a party has come to reasonably rely on the perception, caused by the other party, that there is a 'deal' or at least a preliminary deal or a commitment from the other party that could be perceived of as an intention to conclude a contract.

203. Precontractual liability limits the freedom of contract in order to protect the 'reasonable reliance' on a promise and this is expressed as a duty to negotiate in good faith.

B. *Culpa in Contrahendo*

204. Precontractual liability is a general norm concerning the duty of care consisting of a reasonable duty to take the other party's interest into consideration. It is also described as a protection of a party's justifiable reliance on the other party's behaviour/statements during the negotiations. It builds on the concept of 'loyalty', which, generally speaking, means that a negotiating party has a reasonable duty to notify, to disclose information, to limit your loss, to cooperate, etc. Precontractual liability presupposes fault/culpa which means at least negligence, i.e., the party must have deviated from the reasonable standards of care and fairness expected in the circumstances. Usages and practices of the trade or profession can often be used to set the standard for what is reasonable.

205. *Culpa in contrahendo* is a concept that covers different types of negligent behaviour during the contract negotiations. It is the fault rule that constitutes the base for the doctrine of precontractual liability but *culpa in contrahendo* can be at hand regardless of whether the negotiations lead to a contract, lead to an invalid contract or lead to no contract at all. In other words, *culpa in contrahendo*, as a fault rule, exits both in precontractual and in contractual situations.

C. *Duty to Inform*

206. The disclosure of information is one of the most important issues in negotiations. A party has the right to take advantage of a good business opportunity and has no general obligation to submit information to the other party; as a general rule each party is under a duty to keep himself informed about the transaction. However, a party who knows or has reason to believe that the other party lacks information that is essential for the transaction, is (most likely) under a duty to properly disclose that information to the other contracting party. Each party is under a general duty to disclose information that is clearly of importance for the other party's decision to enter into the contract, if the other party is unable to procure that information himself and the non-disclosing party is aware of that fact.

207. A party may not make a false representation about the subject matter which is negotiated in the contract. If the non-disclosure of relevant information is not fraudulent or the result of dishonesty or negligence it is, as a general rule, lawful.[104]

D. *Intention to Contract*

208. In Swedish law, as in other civil law jurisdictions, entering into contract negotiations without having an intention to reach a contract is considered a breach of the duty to bargain in good faith. If during contract negotiations a party determines not to enter into a contract, it must immediately inform the other party that it no longer has an intention to contract. If it does not do so and if, by not doing so, it induces the other party to have expenditures or make reliance investments that turn out to be unnecessary, its conduct might be seen as *culpa in contrahendo* and it might be liable for reliance damages.

E. *Damage*

209. Damages for breach of the precontractual duty to bargain in good faith can only be awarded if the party has suffered loss in terms of wasted time and/or money. The loss corresponds to the 'sunk costs' or 'reliance investments' which the aggrieved party has had as a result of the negotiations, often in order to be well prepared for the deal once it is finally settled. Compensation is limited to the reliance interest, i.e., the aggrieved party has the right to be put in the same position as he would have been in had the expenses for the (potential) deal not been incurred by the other party's culpa.

F. *Summary of Precontractual Liability*

210. The Swedish doctrine of precontractual liability is not a clear-cut doctrine, since there is no general legislation and only a limited number of cases.damages for precontractual liability has in fact only been awarded once (NJA 1963 p. 105).

104. See O. Svensson, Avtalsfrihet och rättvisa, p. 231 (2012).

Chapter 2. Conditions of Substantive Validity

§1. Invalidity/Introduction

211. A contract may be void or declared invalid after a claim for invalidity and it can be invalid in total or only partially. It can be void or voidable due to factors relating to *the parties*, to *the process* that lead to the conclusion of the contract or to *the content* of the contract. The general principles on invalidity are based on legal doctrine and court cases balancing the conflicting interests of the parties against the prevailing interests of the society in a pragmatic fashion.[105]

212. A void contract does not have effect according to its content and it cannot be legally enforced. It does not create any obligations or rights between the parties. It is invalid from the beginning (*ex tunc*). It is considered to be a *nullity*.

213. A contract could be void due to *defects related to the persons*, for instance, when one of the parties did not have the legal capacity to contract. Lack of proper age and disturbed mental status are circumstances which might render a contract void. A related question is the case where the party lacks legal title to the assets regarding which he contracts. If a person enters into a contract whereby, for instance, he sells goods which he does not own and does not have the owner's permission to sell, and the other party knows, or ought to suspect from the circumstances of the transaction that the seller is not the owner, the contract is not enforceable, but rather than seeing the contract as void (providing for damages up to the reliance interest), under Swedish law this situation is seen as an initial breach of contract (providing for damages up to the expectation interest). In this case, the other party's awareness/suspicion of the lack of ownership is determinant for the enforceability of the contract. If, on the contrary, the other party does not know and ought not to have suspected the lack of ownership, he is in good faith (Sw: *i god tro*) and, usually, this makes the contract valid. Cases dealing with the lack of power over assets of which the party disposes, should be distinguished from cases regarding lack of capacity. Lack of title is in Swedish law rather dealt with as a matter of delivery of defect goods.[106]

214. Defects pertaining to the process in which the contract came about, for instance duress or forgery, may make the contract void.

215. In regard to content, a contract which is contrary to mandatory law is invalid in total or partially *ex tunc* and the same, in principle, applies for contracts that are against public policy or morality. If written form is required and the form requirement is not met, the contract is void, an agreement that does not meet these requirements does not constitute a valid contract; it is void from the beginning.

105. See J. Kleineman, De offentliga rättssubjektens avtalskompetens, JT 1994/95 p. 958.
106. See Adlercreutz & Gorton I, p. 250.

216. If the contract is invalid, the effect as a main rule arises *ex tunc*. The parties shall as a main rule make restitution of what they have received under the contract and they have no future rights or obligations under the contract. Where performance has been made and reversal of the performance is not possible, damages may be awarded in lieu of the value of restitution. When no performance has been made, the innocent party may claim compensation for the costs for entering into the invalid contract; reliance interest (Sw: *negativa kontraktsintresset*).[107]

217. Invalidity issues may arise under section 36 of the Contracts Act in particular when a clause is deemed to be unreasonable. When such clause is stricked out, the consequence may be that the whole contract should be set aside. In this case it can be said that the contract is declared void *ex nunc*. It should be noted that the setting aside under section 36 applies to initial as well as subsequent circumstances, whereas the general principles on invalidity only encompasses initial circumstances, i.e., circumstances that were at hand when the contract was concluded.

I. General Remarks

218. Although the so-called invalidity catalogue found in sections 28–33 of the Contracts Act with one exception regard invalidity due to defects of will, the general doctrine of invalidity cannot be said to be based on a subjective will theory as the case might be in many civil law systems.[108] Section 36 of the Contracts Act, according to which a contract can be modified to the point where the whole contract is set aside has been influential and has further opened up for a pragmatic approach to invalidity and the consequences of invalidity.

219. A contract may be invalid for many other reasons than the ones stated in the invalidity catalogue. Often the invalidity issue is determined by what is considered fair in terms of legal consequences. Declaring a contract void usually means restitution of performance and that the contract does not have any legal effects with regard to the future but it may very well have legal effects in terms of a right to damages (mostly only to the reliance interest) for a party in good faith when such a solution is considered justified. The legal consequences of invalidity vary and cannot be said to follow any distinct pattern. The overall purpose of letting invalid contracts have consequences in the form of damages is the promotion of a well-functioning economic market.[109]

220. Invalidity is regarded as a complex part of contract law where Swedish law seems to differ from civil law systems and common law. Since there is no civil code and no legislative systematic approach to invalidity in Swedish law, statutory provisions on invalidity are scattered. Provisions are to be found e.g., in the Act on

107. See also s. 6.
108. See e.g., Sefton-Green, R. [ed.], Mistake, Fraud and Duties to Inform in European Contract Law, p. 3 (2005).
109. See T. Ingvarsson, Ogiltighet och rättsföljd, p. 79 (2012).

Instruments of Debt (Sw: Lag 1936:81 om skuldebrev), the Competition Act (Sw Konkurrenslagen 2008:579), the Commission Agency Act (Sw Kommissionslagen 2009:865), the Commercial Agency Act (Sw: Lag 1991:351 om handelsagentur), the Bankruptcy Act (Sw: Konkurslagen 1987:672) and the Consumer Sales Act (Sw: Konsumentköplagen 1990:932). Such provisions regard invalidity in respect of many different situations which all call for various attempts to balance the typical interests at hand.

II. Voidness and Voidability

221. Legal doctrine has established a distinction between *absolute voidness* ('strong invalidity') and *voidability* ('weak invalidity'). In principle, a *void* legal act or a void contract does not have effect according to its content and it cannot be legally enforced. It is considered to be a nullity with effect *ex tunc*. Nullity is (1) self-executing and absolute, it shall (2) be recognized ex officio by courts and other public authorities, it can (3) be invoked by everybody who has a legal interest of some kind related to the void contract, it is (4) definite and not possible to heal and it (5) has effect even if the other party is in good faith, i.e., he was neither aware of nor ought to have been aware of the fact which made the contract void.

222. A *voidable* contract is a contract which can be declared invalid due to some defect related to the contract from the beginning but the ground for invalidity is not as strong as is the case with automatically void contracts. The distinction between voidness and voidability is not always clear. A voidable contract must be annulled on the initiative of the other party and this party must give notice within reasonable time from his becoming aware of the fact which makes the contract voidable. If no initiative to declare the contract void is taken, the voidable contract remains in force and performance shall take place in accordance with the contract.

223. Circumstances pertaining to the negotiations and the conclusion of the contract may render a contract voidable, for instance if one of the parties was negligent during the negotiations (*culpa in contrahendo*), or, there was undue influence, fraud or misrepresentation on the side of a contracting party. Mistake might render a contract voidable, i.e., when there has not been a 'meeting of the minds' and hence no valid agreement between the parties. If the contract is voidable, the 'innocent' party must claim that it is avoided, otherwise it remains in force. The lack of any such claim as well as sheer passivity from the side of the innocent party will 'heal' the grounds for voidability. If the innocent party explicitly refrains from claiming avoidance after it has become aware of the circumstance that makes the contract voidable, it can no longer claim avoidance. A contract will not be declared void if the other party was not aware of or ought not to have been aware of the ground for invalidity. The party is then said to have been in good faith (Sw: *i god tro*). If the contract is avoided, it is invalid from the beginning and the rights and obligations that were intended to be created should be treated as if they had never occurred; the parties shall, in principle, make restitution of what they have received under the contract and they have no future rights or obligations under the contract. Where restitution of performance is not possible, damages amounting to the reliance interest may be rewarded as compensation.

III. Contracts Where Not All of the Terms Have Been Agreed

224. Even if the parties have not agreed on all terms, a court may fill out the gaps given that a sufficiently clear default provision is at hand. Such default provisions may be found in statutory law; e.g., section 45 of the Sale of Goods Act providing for the buyer to pay a price that is reasonable with regard to the kind of goods concerned, the common price for the goods at the time of the contract 'and other circumstances'. The last set of factors gives the court a margin of appreciation. If the parties on the other hand have not agreed on the quantity (i.e., an agreement on quantity cannot be construed by means of interpretation), the 'contract' is deemed to be incomplete and hence disregarded.

IV. The Doctrine of Impossibility

225. The Roman law principle of impossibility (*impossibilum nulla obligatio est*) is not seen as a special doctrine in Swedish contract law. The fact that, already at the time of the conclusion of the contract, the performance of the obligation assumed was impossible, does not render the contract void. Here, Swedish law is more in accordance with the UNIDROIT Principle, Article 3.3 which states that the mere fact that at the time of the conclusion of the contract the performance of the obligation assumed was impossible does not affect the validity of the contract. Initial impossibility of performance is normally seen as equal to impossibility occurring after the conclusion of the contract and is dealt with as a matter of non-performance.[110]

V. General Remarks About Formalities

226. If there are formal requirements for establishing a valid contract, for instance if written form is required, an agreement that does not meet these requirements does not constitute a contract; it is void from the beginning. The fact that a party to a (void) contract was not aware of the existence of the invalidity ground does not matter; the contract is automatically void.

227. Swedish contract law is not characterized by a high degree of formality. In other legal systems there are requirements regarding formalities, for instance the participation or confirmation of a public official in the form of a notary, in order to make the contract valid. No such requirements exist in Swedish contract law.[111]

110. See also s. 4 III.
111. See further Introduction to the Law of Contracts s. 6 III and Part I Ch. 1 M.

VI. The General Clause on the Modification/Setting Aside of Contracts

228. In Sweden, issues of invalidity, or rather annulment of a contract is most often dealt with under the general clause in section 36 of the Contracts Act on the modification of contracts due to unreasonableness, i.e., section 36 of the Contracts Act. This clause was introduced in Chapter 3 on Invalidity of the Contracts Act in 1976. The application of the clause has to a large extent replaced the use of the special invalidity rules.

229. The clause provides for the modification or setting aside of unreasonable contract terms and makes it possible to modify one or more contract terms and the contract as such to the point where the whole contract is set aside. Setting aside the whole contract amounts to declaring the whole contract void. However, in such a case the contract is not void from its beginning, *ab initio*, but from the time when the court declares the contract to be set aside, *ex nunc*.

230. The clause has had its main area of applicability in consumer contracts. It has been applied to standard contractual terms which have not been individually negotiated that have been deemed contrary to the requirement of good faith or to cause a significant imbalance in the parties' rights and obligations to the detriment of the consumer.[112] The clause has however also been applied to modify or set aside individually negotiated contracts or contract terms which are considered unreasonable.

231. The clause has also been used to modify contracts between commercial parties. In several cases, arbitration clauses in contracts between commercial actors and consumers have been declared invalid since they have been regarded unreasonable (unreasonably expensive, for instance) for the consumer. In other cases contract terms or whole contracts have been avoided due to hardship/changing circumstances. The right for one party to unilaterally change the terms of a contract has also been considered unreasonable.

232. Whether a term is unreasonable or not shall be determined from the content of the entire contract, from the circumstances prevailing at the conclusion of the contract as well as subsequent circumstances and circumstances in general.

§2. Capacity of the Parties

I. Minors

233. A person must have legal capacity in order to be able to enter into a valid contract. The rules concerning legal capacity make no distinction between men and women or between Swedish citizens and foreign nationals. However, age matters. As a general rule, a person under the age of 18 (a minor) does not have capacity to

112. Compare Art. 3(1) of EU Directive 93/13.

perform legal acts. If a person under the age of 18 enters into a contract, in principle, the contract is void. If a contract (with a minor) is properly performed it cannot afterwards be declared void. If a minor performs a legal act which falls outside of his legal capacity, his act may afterwards be confirmed by his guardian (Sw: *förmyndare*) and in such a case the legal act, for instance a contract, is valid from its inception (*ab initio*). A party who enters into a contract with a minor, knowing that he is contracting with a minor, may not revoke his legal act until a reasonable time has passed during which the guardian shall have an opportunity to confirm the contract. Chapter 9 section 1 of the Swedish Code on Parenthood (Sw: *Föräldrabalken 1949:381*) states that, as a general rule, a minor is not entitled to handle his own property or take upon himself any obligations. Only in cases explicitly spelled out in the following text of the same section may a minor perform legally binding acts. All of these situations shall not be enumerated here, but the main purpose of the regulation is to protect the minor.

234. All persons above the age of eighteen have legal capacity if they have not been deprived of this capacity or parts of this capacity by law. Legal capacity implies, among other things, that the person has the right to perform legal acts, for instance to enter into valid contracts.

235. From the age of sixteen, a minor may contract regarding property which he has earned through his own work. If a minor has his own household, he is allowed to contract with regard to the regular needs if his everyday household and for bringing up of children living in the same household. A minor who runs a business with proper permission from his *guardian(-s)* has the right to enter into contracts related to his business. A minor may enter into an employment contract with the permission of his caretaker(-s) and, at the age of sixteen, he may terminate the contract by himself and enter into a new employment of a similar kind without having to ask for his caretaker's permission. Usually, if the minor's parents are married to each other, together they are the caretakers of the child and also the child's guardians.

236. If the contract with the minor is avoided, the consequence is restitution or, if this is not possible, damages. The minor is only obliged to pay damages for what has been used for his maintenance or for what has been of use for him. If the minor has given false information about his legal capacity which has deceived the other party or if the minor has acted in a criminal way, his duty to pay damages is more severe. However, his duty to pay damages never exceeds the reliance interest (Sw: *negativa kontraktsintresset*).

II. Insanity or Other Mental Disturbances

237. Severe lack of mental capacity may also make a party unable to enter into a contract. Under the Act (1924:323) regarding the effects of contract concluded under the influence of mental disturbance, such a contract is void and the parties should make restitution by returning the benefits that they may have received under the contract or, if this is not possible, pay compensation for the value of the benefit.

However, the party with the mental disturbance is only liable to pay for what has been of use (Sw: *nytta*) for it. If the other party did not know or ought not to have known that the first party entered into the contract under the influence of such a mental disturbance, it has a right to be compensated for its loss to a reasonable extent. It is noteworthy that temporary mental disturbances due to chock, intoxication, extreme fright, etc. might also constitute the type of mental condition that may render a contract void under this statute.

238. If a person who has reached the age of eighteen, as a result of sickness, psychiatric disturbance, weak health conditions or similar reasons, needs help to protect his rights and take care of his property, the court can appoint a custodian (Sw: *god man*). In the case of more serious disturbances, if the person in question is unable to take care of himself or his property, the court might appoint a trustee (Sw: *förvaltare*). In those cases the person in question has limited legal capacity to enter into contracts by himself but very seldom is he deprived of that capacity altogether. Usually, he still has the right – without the participation of the trustee – to take employment, to make use of money/property which he has earned through his own work and to use gifts and a few other kinds of property which he has received or earned.

III. Married Women. Aliens

239. With regard to the concept of legal capacity, there is no difference between men and women or between Swedes and citizens of other countries.

IV. Bankruptcy

240. A person who is in bankruptcy does not have the legal right to enter into contracts about his assets/property. His legal rights as owner to his assets are taken over by an external bankruptcy manager.

V. Moral Person

241. The concept 'moral person' does not exist in Swedish law.

§3. Defects in Consent

I. General Remarks

242. As has already been mentioned, Swedish contract law does not rest so clearly on the theory of defects in consent as seems to be the case of many other European civil law systems. However, the 'invalidity catalogue' in Chapter 3, sections 28–33 of the Contracts Act, contains four types of situations where a contract is either automatically void or may be declared void as a result of defects in consent. These are grounds for invalidity found in most jurisdiction, i.e., the conclusion of a contract under the pressure of violence/duress/coercion (sections 28 and 29), as a result of fraud (section 30), usury (section 31) and mistake (section 32). Section 33 also contains rules about grounds for invalidity but that section is not a clear defects in consent rule. It deals with the effects of dishonest behaviour at the conclusion of a contract. All sections of the 'invalidity catalogue' refer to behaviour at the time of the conclusion of the contract, not necessarily behaviour by the other party but also behaviour by a third party. Sections 28–31 have their equivalents in the Swedish Penal Code, sections 28 and 29 about violence (robbery, blackmail), section 30 about fraud (criminal fraud), section 31 about usury (criminal usury).

II. The Doctrine of Failed Assumptions

243. Mention should be made of a special doctrine building on the theory of defects in consent/mistake which is not found in the Contracts Act or any other statute. The doctrine could in English be called *the doctrine of failed (contractual) assumptions* (Sw: *förutsättningsläran*). It is a doctrine which has been developed through case law and legal doctrine. It is seen as complementary to both the doctrine of contract interpretation and the doctrine of invalidity. It forms part of the more general doctrine of mistake but it has been chiseled out as a special doctrine regarding mistake built on *error in motivis*. It covers both assumptions at the time of the conclusion of the contract (failed assumptions, Sw: *oriktiga förutsättningar*) and assumptions that later turn out to be wrong ('subsequently failed assumptions', Sw: *bristande förutsättningar*).

244. The doctrine of failed assumptions is not a clear cut doctrine but could in general terms be described as follows. A contract may be declared void if (1) one of the parties made a fundamental assumption when it entered into the contract and this assumption was a reason for its entering into the contract and if (2) the other party was aware of this assumption, also with regard to its significance for the first party, and if (3) this assumption turns out to either be false or fails due to already existing circumstances or to circumstances which occurred after the contract was concluded and if (4) it seems reasonable to put the risk for the false/failed assumption on the other party. According to the general rule in contract law, each party, when entering into a contract, stands the risk of its own assumptions failing.

245. However, in exceptional cases, it might be reasonable and fair to let the other party carry that risk. This can only happen when the other party has behaved negligent in some way or when circumstances change in a way that makes it reasonable to let the other party carry the risk for the failed assumption. The assumption can be seen as an implicit contract term. However, if the assumption has been spelled out in the form of an explicit term in the contract, the doctrine of failed assumptions does not apply. If a contract term is not fulfilled/performed, the failure might rather be a question of breach of contract than a question of avoiding the contract. If a contract is declared void under the doctrine of failed assumptions the consequence is usually restitution. However, since the doctrine is seen not only as an invalidity doctrine but also as complementary to the doctrine of interpretation, the court may also use the doctrine of failed assumptions to decide how the content of the contractual relationship between the party should be understood, for instance with regard to the price of the goods or services in a transaction.

III. Duress, Coercion, Undue Influence

246. Section 28, paragraph 1 of the Contracts Act deals with legal acts performed under the pressure of physical violence or severe threat against the party. Such a legal act is invalid and a contract entered into through such a legal act is always void.

247. Paragraph 2 of the same section also deals with duress but refers to a different situation; in this case the contract is voidable, i.e., it has to be claimed invalid by somebody (the person who has been subject to duress). It refers to a situation where there are at least three persons involved and the person who is subject to duress, B, enters into a contract – as a result of the duress – with a party, C, who is not aware of and ought not to be aware of the duress exerted on the other contracting party by a third party, A. Once the duress has ceased, B must 'without unreasonable delay' notify C that he, B, was under threat from A when entering into the contract and that he, B, wants to have the contract rescinded. If B does not do this the contract is binding.

248. A person who performs a legal act under duress is considered to not act in accordance with his will; he is not giving his consent to the legal act he is forced to perform. In other words, the contract does not express the true intention of the party and thus – according to the will principle – is not valid.

249. Section 29 deals with coercion, a weaker form of duress or undue influence but still a behaviour that can render a contract void. Duress is harsher than undue influence (which is a common law doctrine) but both concepts have to do with the use of illegitimate pressure in order to make a person enter into a contract.

250. Section 29 refers to a form of blackmail situation or a situation where a contract has been induced by one party's illegitimate pressure on the other. If a person is coerced to perform a legal act, that act is not legally valid if the coercion is exerted by the other party to the contract or if this party knows or ought to know that the first party is entering into the contract as a result of coercion exerted by a third person.

IV. Fraud

251. Fraud is another situation where a contract may be void as a result of defects of consent. It is regulated in section 30 of the Contracts Act. A contract which has come about as the result of fraud is void since the legal act performed by the party which has been fraudulently deceived is not binding. The person exerting the fraud must be aware of the fact that he is deceiving the other party by giving false factual information or by not giving such information. In addition, he must be aware of the fact that the other party does not know of the facts in question. The fraudulent act must be the cause of the legal act performed by the other party. This requirement might make it difficult to prove that non-disclosure, i.e., silence, is a fraudulent behaviour.

V. Usury (Unfair Exploitation)

252. Section 31 of the Contracts Act deals with usury. Usury means exploitation of another person's financial or personal distress, dependency, etc. at the conclusion of the contract. In a comparative perspective, usury can be compared to the common law doctrine of undue influence, particularly when the exploitation/pressure involves abuse of a position of trust or confidence resulting in a stronger party achieving a contract with a weaker party. A contract which has come about through usury is not binding for the exploited person.

253. An example of usury can be, for instance, when a lender exploits the financial distress of a borrower in order to get an interest rate on the loan which manifestly exceeds the normal interest rate.

VI. Mistake

A. Mistake in the Declaration of Intent

254. Whereas in the continental civil law systems a contract may be invalid due to mistake in a wide range of situations, the Swedish Contracts Act mainly deals with mistake in the situation where there is a mistake in the expression or transmission of a statement or a text. One type of mistake is when a party's statement does not correspond with its actual intent; it is making an error in its declaration of intent. Another situation is when a party, entering into a contract, gives its statement the intended content but is mistaken with regard to the circumstances that lie behind its statement of intent; it is a case of *error in motivis.*

255. When there is a mistake in the sense that the 'internal will' of a party does not correspond with the external declaration of its will, there is no consent, no actual 'meeting of the minds' which formally, according to the will theory, is required for there to be a contract. In principle, Swedish contract law in these cases of mistake primarily protects the reasonable reliance of the other party.

256. The Swedish Contracts Act explicitly deals with the first situation, mistake in the declaration of intent (Sw: *förklaringsmisstag*). Section 32, paragraph 1 of the Contracts Act reads as follows:

> Where any person provides a statement of intent which, as a result of a typographical error or other mistake on his part, imparts different meaning than the one intended, such person shall not be bound by the statement of intent if the party to whom it was addressed realized, or should have realized, the mistake.

257. The erroneous statement/the legal act is binding for the person who makes the mistake if the other party is in good faith when it takes notice of the statement, i.e., did not realize or ought not to have realized that the other party's real intent was not in accordance with its statement. This means that the contract becomes valid in spite of the fact that it has been given a content which the mistaken party did not intend. The contrary is true if the party receiving the erroneous statement was in bad faith, i.e., understood or ought to have understood that the other party was mistaken. The mistake may consist in an error in a written document, a misrepresentation or any other type of error caused by the party itself in the bringing over of the statement of intent to the other party.

258. With regard to this type of mistake, Swedish law does not reflect the 'will principle' (i.e., it is not the will/intent of the party that determines the content of the legal act) but instead 'the reasonable reliance' principle. If the other party has no reason to believe that there was something wrong with the statement, his reasonable reliance on the message is the determinant factor and the statement is considered a valid legal act which, for instance, can lead to a contract. The recognition of this principle (and not the will principle) is considered good for the functioning of the market economy where the possibility to rely on offers, bids and statements in general between merchants is considered conducive to efficient economic transactions.

259. In the situation where the party who has made a statement of intent which has been distorted during transport due to factors independent of himself, that party is not bound by the distorted statement. If he does not want to be bound he is obliged to notify the recipient 'without unreasonable delay' once he learns about the distortion. When contracting over the Internet the same rules apply.

B. Mistake as to the Person

260. Usually a party to a contract is well aware of the identity of the other party. However, there are situations when it might be unclear who is actually becoming bound by a contract. Commercial intermediaries of various kinds represent other persons, legal as well as physical. A company limited by shares can be represented by the chief executive operator (CEO) without any specific mandate from the board of the company; his or her mandate follows directly from the Company Act. If it is not made clear – or is considered obvious from the circumstances – whether a person enters into the contract in his/her own name or on behalf of the company, the main rule is that a person is entering into the contract on his/her own behalf, i.e., in his/her capacity as a physical person. If an agent enters into a contract on behalf of his principal but without authority to bind the principal, the contract is void but the agent might in such a case be liable for the expectation interest towards the third party if the agent has given the impression that he had a proper authority from his principal (section 25 of the Contracts Act). Thus, an agent who acts – without mandate – for his principal never becomes bound by the contract himself; instead he might be liable to pay damages to the third party.

C. Mistake as to the Substance

261. Mistake as to substance is at hand in the case where there is a mistake with regard to the type of contract entered into (sale instead of lease) or with regard to the goods of the transaction (apples instead of pears). Whereas in many civil law countries such cases are dealt with under contract law, in Sweden they are usually dealt with as a matter of breach of the obligations assumed under the contract, for instance, in the case of a sales contract, under the specific rules on 'fault' in the Sale of Goods Act. To be accepted as a mistake as to substance under contract law, the mistaken party must show that the mistake was so serious that it would not have entered into the contract had it known the truth and, in addition, it must show that the other party understood or ought to have understood that the issue was important to the first party at the conclusion of the contract. If a party can choose between having the contract declared void due to mistake or terminating the contract due to breach, it is up to the party starting the court procedure to decide which legal ground to choose but – under Swedish law – it will (probably) never get higher compensation/damages than follows from termination due to breach, i.e., the expectation interest at the most.[113]

VII. The General Clause on Dishonesty

262. The moral duty to act honestly is the basis for section 33 of the Contracts Act which is construed as a widely applicable rule of invalidity. Before the general clause in section 36 of the Contracts Act was introduced in 1976, section 33 was the general principle of invalidity and it was intended to be the last resort for declaring a contract invalid in cases where it would be against honesty and good faith to rely on the legal act or the contract. It was designed to cover cases which were not covered by the other, more specific, invalidity rules of the Contracts Act. Today after the arrival of the extensive general clause in section 36, it is much less used and some consider that it could be abolished altogether. However, section 33 which has to do with honesty and good faith, is not fully covered by section 36 which has to do with reasonableness, and therefore section 33 is still on the statute book, now called the small general clause on invalidity (contrary to section 36 which is called the big general clause).

263. Like the other invalidity rules in the 'invalidity catalogue' section 33 refers to the time of conclusion of the contract; circumstances that happen later cannot

113. See T. Ingvarsson, Ogiltighet och rättsföljd, pp 80–86 (2012).

cause the contract to be declared void. In this respect there is an important difference between section 33 and section 36, since the latter also covers subsequent circumstances.

264. Section 33 is a so-called general clause which means that it has a broad application It actually covers all the situations that are specially regulated in sections 28–31.

265. Section 33 covers the case where a party acts dishonestly against the other party by using the prevailing circumstances in an inequitable way, i.e., in a way which is against good faith and fair dealing (Sw: *i strid med tro och heder*) when it performs the legal act, fully aware of the fact that its behaviour is against good faith and fair dealing. The dishonesty also pertains to the party's intention to 'rely on' the legal act in question. Under section 33, such a legal act may not 'be relied upon' which is to say that it does not create a binding contract. The rule requires that the acting party knows or 'must be presumed' to have known the relevant circumstances at the time when the contract was concluded; if he gets to know these circumstances later, section 33 does not apply and the contract cannot be declared void. An example of a situation in which section 33 might be applied is the case where the first party knows that a certain piece of art, owned by an old person not very knowledgeable about art, is much more worth than what the owner, the other party, believes and the first party does not tell the owner the truth but, instead, in taking advantage of the old person's lack of knowledge, buys the piece of art for a price way below its actual value.

266. Section 33 is very seldom used today since section 36 has now more or less taken over as the general clause for contract modification and contract avoidance.

VIII. Misrepresentation

267. The common law doctrine of misrepresentation does not have a directly corresponding equivalent in Swedish law. Misrepresentation implies making false statements in contract negotiations. If the other party was induced to enter into the contract as a result of these statements – since that party believes them to be true – and the statements become part of the contract, this constitutes misrepresentation providing the other party a right to various remedies. Under English Common Law, regardless of whether the statements were made fraudulently, carelessly or totally innocently, they make the contract voidable for misrepresentation.[114]

268. Even if no comparable specific doctrine of misrepresentation is found in Swedish law, no doubt, there are similar rules in various regulations and in case law, aiming at the same result. Under Swedish law, there is no clear distinction between

---

114. See J. Cartwright, Contract Law. An Introduction to the English Law of Contract for the Civil Lawyer, p. 161 (2007).

actual misrepresentation (in the Common Law sense) and the duty to inform/non-disclosure during contract negotiations. If a party makes a statement of fact during contract negotiations, such a statement can sometimes constitute a guarantee and in such a case, if the parties arrive at the contract, the party is strictly liable for the accuracy of its statement.

269. An explicit obligation to provide full and accurate information to the other party at the conclusion of the contract is stipulated in various pieces of legislation covering different types of contract. For instance, The Insurance Contracts Act (2005:104) prescribes a far-reaching duty to inform, for the insurer in the case of consumer insurance and insurance of persons, and for the insured a general duty to provide the insurer with full and accurate information. Fraudulent non-disclosure or misrepresentation from the insured may render the insurance contract void. Negligent non-disclosure and misrepresentation by the insured may result in the indemnity being reduced in proportion to how the risk has been mis-calculated due to the non-disclosure/misrepresentation.

270. Another example is the seller's obligation to provide information to the buyer under the Sale of Goods Act and under the special consumer protection regulation. Section 18, first paragraph, of the Sale of Goods Act puts on the seller a duty to perform, i.e., deliver the merchandise, in accordance with what has been said about the characteristics and use of the merchandise in the marketing of the merchandise or in information provided by the seller himself before the purchase, if such representation can be considered to have influenced the purchase. Otherwise the goods/merchandise is considered to be defective. If the seller's statement is false, the merchandise is considered to be defective regardless of whether the seller knew or ought to have known that his (or his representative's) statement was false. The remedies for the buyer are those provided by the Sale of Goods Act but the buyer may also use contract law to claim damages, to rescind the contract term or the whole contract, etc. General 'sales talk' or general praise of the merchandise from the side of the seller does not make the seller liable under section 18 of the Sales of Goods Act. An even more far-reaching duty to inform is put on the seller in regulation regarding the seller's transactions with consumers, see, for instance, section 16 of the Consumer Sales Act and sections 13 and 14 of the Product Liability Act (the latter also including information duties on the producer).

271. From case law a much discussed Supreme Court case regarding misrepresentation/the duty to inform should be mentioned (NJA 2007 p. 86). In that case a contract regarding the sale of real estate property was rescinded as a result of the seller not providing enough information about the property. The real estate was an attractive, seaside piece of property intended by the buyer to be used as his summer resort. However, close to the property but out of sight from it, there was a motocross training site which caused lots of noise and disturbance for the neighbourhood when it was in use. The seller did not inform the buyer about the motocross site and the buyer did not investigate the neighbourhood. Only a couple of months after the contract was completed and the price paid, the buyer terminated (Sw:*hävde*) the contract due to the disturbance from the motocross site. It turned out that the seller – while he owned the property – had himself been in contact several times with the municipality in order to have the motocross training limited to hours when it would not disturb the surroundings so much; in other words, the seller was well aware of the disturbance from the motocross activity but he had not informed the buyer about this before the contract was concluded. The main question in the case was whether the seller had fulfilled his duty to inform or whether the buyer had fulfilled his duty to investigate the premises (and the neighbourhood) before the purchase. The Supreme Court held that the contract should be avoided since the seller, who knew about the noise from the motocross site, must have understood that the absence of such noise was of fundamental importance for the buyer, who wanted to find a peaceful place for his summer resort. According to the Court, the seller must have understood that the buyer did not know anything about the existence of the motocross site and the noise and the seller had, thus, taken advantage of the buyer's lack of information in a way which gave the buyer a right to rescind the contract.

272. Carelessly or innocently made false statements which have become part of the contract and which are believed to be true by the other party who was induced to enter into the contract as a result of the false statements, may render the contract, or the particular contract term, void under the general clause in section 36 of the Contracts Act. In a recent, already famous, Norwegian case, section 36 of the Norwegian Contracts Act (which in relevant parts is similar to section 36 of the Swedish Contracts Act) was used to rescind a contract between a bank and a consumer regarding an investment by the consumer in a financial product of a rather complicated sort (in Norwegian: *aksjeindeksobligasjon*). The fact that the bank misrepresented the facts about the possible revenue of the product was an important reason (in addition to the uneven bargaining power and the complexity of the product) for the Norwegian Supreme Court to rescind the contract and award damages to the consumer. The Court further explained that this was the result regardless of whether the bank had been in good or bad faith; it was enough that the represented facts were objectively false.[115,116] However, in order for section 36 of the Contracts Act to be applicable, it is not enough that the false statements have become part of the contract. It is necessary to find the contract term or the contract as a whole unconscionable (Sw: *oskäligt)* as a result of the misrepresentation.

273. The doctrine of failed assumptions may also be applied to vitiate a contract in situations of misrepresentation where the other party has entered into the contract relying on the represented facts and the court finds it justified to rescind the contract as a result of the misrepresentation. This may be the case even in situations where the party making the misrepresentation believed the facts to be true. (NJA 1985 p. 178).

115. See Rt. 2013 p. 388, the so-called Røeggen case.
116. See also J. Giertsen, Avtaler, pp 241 et seq. (2014).

IX. Gross Disparity

274. In the situation where there is gross disparity between the obligations of the contract parties, if none of the particular invalidity clauses in the Contracts Act apply, it might be possible to modify or terminate the contract (or the contract term) under the general clause in section 36 of the Contracts Act. This clause covers both the conditions at the time of the conclusion of the contract and conditions which have occurred later. For adaptation or termination to be available, the contract or the contract term must be unconscionable In the determination of whether this is the case, special regard should be given to the relationship between the parties and protection be given to the weaker party, if it is, for instance, a consumer.

275. In cases of gross disparity, there is no doctrine of hardship in Swedish law, similar to the one found in the UNIDROIT Principles Chapter 6, section 2, which gives the disadvantaged party a right to renegotiations. However, such a right is often provided in Swedish standard form contracts.[117]

§4. OTHER CONDITIONS OF VALIDITY

I. Existing and Lawful Cause

276. There is no theory on existing and lawful cause (that a contractual obligation must have a cause and that that the cause must be legal) in Swedish contract law. The problem which the cause doctrine tries to solve is, in Nordic legal systems, resolved through procedural rules and rules regarding the burden of proof.[118]

II. Initial Impossibility

277. The Roman law principle of impossibility (*impossibilum nulla obligatio est*) is not seen as a special doctrine under Swedish contract law. The fact that, already at the time of the conclusion of the contract, the performance of the obligation assumed was impossible, does not render the contract void. Here, Swedish law is more in accordance with the UNIDROIT Principle, Article 3.3 which states that the mere fact that at the time of the conclusion of the contract, the performance of the obligation assumed was impossible, does not affect the validity of the contract. Initial impossibility of performance is normally seen as equal to impossibility occurring after the conclusion of the contract and is dealt with as a matter of non-performance.

117. See U. Bernitz, Standardavtalsrätt, p. 82 (2013).
118. See H. Ussing, Aftaler paa formuerettens omraade, p. 114 (1950). See also III below.

III. Contracts Against Public Policy

278. Contracts for illegal purposes are deemed to be void. The same is the case for contracts which are against mandatory regulation, for instance cartel agreements are forbidden and void under the Competition Act. The same applies to contracts that are against mandatory consumer protection regulation and employment contracts which do not recognize the mandatory rules aimed at the protection of the employee.

279. In case law the courts have dealt with the – not so unusual – question of the validity of contracts, often construction contracts, where the parties have agreed on a price which builds on the explicit assumption between the parties that income tax on the profit shall not be paid and which, in turn, means a lower price for the construction work. On the Swedish market such contracts are called 'black work' contracts. The courts have made it clear that such agreements are not valid since the parties are not free to agree on how income shall be taxed (it is rather a matter for the tax authorities). However, the courts have not refused to deal with such contracts altogether. On the contrary, when the parties have started a dispute about the price, the courts have accepted to admit the case but have decided not to try it in substance or to enforce the contract, for instance by supporting a claim for a higher price (than the one initially agreed by the parties) for the construction work. In one case, the claim for a higher price than the one originally agreed, was a result of the first party's sudden demand for a receipt for his payment (whereby the 'black work' arrangement, and the actual income for the constructor, might become known to the tax authorities).[119]

IV. Contracts Against Morality

280. A contract for immoral purposes (a *pactum turpe*) is, in principle, void. However, this legal ground of invalidity is becoming increasingly difficult to apply as society is becoming more multi-cultural and liberal and moral standards more manifold. Recent case law indicates a tendency towards an accentuation of the need to perform a nuanced evaluation of a contract being deemed illegal or immoral.[120] There is no regulation on *pactum turpe*. A payment promise by a man to a pregnant woman for her undertaking an abortion was not enforced as it was considered against the ethical principles of Swedish law (*pactum turpe*), see Swedish Appellate Court case RH 2004:41. Opposing views exist among Swedish jurists with regard to the question whether payments made before or upon conclusion of contracts considered immoral may be restituted.[121] Gambling debts are usually not considered valid obligations and thus, are not possible to enforce through the courts. However,

---

119. See NJA 2004 p. 682.
120. See J. Munukka, Civil Law Consequences of Corruption in Sweden. Stockholm Centre for Commercial Law Årsbok II, p. 285 (2010), with references to NJA 1989 p. 768; 1992 p. 299; 1997 p. 93; 2002 p. 332 and NJA 2004 p. 682.
121. Munukka, *supra*, p. 285.

at the same time such debts are not seen as non-existent in the sense that if a party pays his gambling debts it is considered a valid payment and they cannot be restituted. In NJA 1989 p. 768, money constituting bets in an illegal poker game were subject to restitution to its owners in a case of compulsory execution. The Supreme Court rejected the view that the legal order should not be used as an aid in such situations.[122]

V. Contracts Against Mandatory Regulation

281. Contracts against mandatory regulation are usually void. Today there exists an extensive regulation protecting the weaker party to a contract and such regulation is usually mandatory. For instance, regulation regarding consumer protection and regulation regarding the employment relationship are usually mandatory and cannot be set aside by contract.

282. Contracts about the transfer of real estate property must, for instance, contain a declaration of the transfer (sale or gift) of the accurately identified property and –in the case of a sales contract – it must also state the price of the property. Furthermore, it must be in writing. If these conditions are not met, the contract is void.

283. Contracts against legal prohibitions (Sw: *legala förbud*) can be declared void if the purpose of the prohibition justifies such a consequence.[123] If that is not the case, a contract against a legal prohibition may very well be legally valid. In the case NJA 1997 p. 93 a party had entered into a commercial contract in spite of the fact that he was under a prohibition to carry out his business (Sw: *näringsförbud*). In the regulation on the prohibition to carry on businesses there was nothing indicating that contracts entered into by a person under such a prohibition should be declared void. The Supreme Court rules that the issue of voidability – in such a case – should be solved in accordance with general principles of law, i.e., the contract should be declared void only if the contract implied that the purpose of the prohibition was frustrated. In the case at hand this was not the situation and, hence, the contract was not invalid.[124]

284. According to the dominant view, building on NJA 1993 p. 93, more explicitly there are four aspects to be taken into account when determining whether a contract entered into against mandatory regulation ought to be declared invalid.[125] Those aspects are (1) the purpose of the legal prohibition, (2) whether declaring the contract invalid is needed for the effectiveness of the prohibition (Sw: *effektiva upprätthållandet*), (3) whether declaring the contract invalid can be considered fair

122. Munukka, *supra*, p. 285.
123. See NJA 1997 p. 93.
124. See J. Kleineman, Allmänna principer för ogiltighetspåföljdens inträdande, JT 1997/98 pp 808 et seq.
125. T. Ingvarsson, Spel och osedliga avtal, SvJT 2004, p. 751.

between the parties, and (4) whether the other party's good or bad faith shall be given any significance.

285. A public authority, for instance a municipality, is not entitled to contract about such public services which can only be offered through public regulation of different kind. Such a service is, for instance, the offering of market space in the public domain.[126]

§5. The Re-integra Rule of Section 39 of the Contracts Act

286. Many of the provisions of the Contract Act refer to a specific point in time when a person's knowledge or good faith should be at hand. For instance, the binding effect of a promise (offer) arises when the promisee has knowledge of the promise (offer). The general principle for the good faith requirement is that a person's good faith ('that he knew or ought to have known' something) should be at hand at the moment when the legal act becomes known to him. However, according to section 39 subsequent knowledge about a fact (e.g., that the offeror does not want to be bound) can be relevant if the offeree has not yet acted in reliance on the offer.[127]

§6. The Legal Consequences of Invalidity

I. General Remarks

287. As aforementioned under §1 the consequences of invalidity as a main rule arise *ex tunc* and the parties shall make restitution of what they have received under the contract. Where performance has been made and reversal of the performance is not possible, damages may be awarded in lieu of the value of restitution. When no performance has been made, the innocent party may claim compensation for the costs for entering into the invalid contract; reliance interest (Sw: *negativa kontraktsintresset*).

II. Avoidance of the Contract. Nullity

288. Nullity of a contract may be invoked by everybody with a legal interest in the matter and absolute nullity, as a principle (with many exceptions), can never be 'healed'. See §2 above. Avoidance of a voidable contract can be invoked by the 'innocent' party of the contract by giving notice to the other party within a reasonable time after he has become aware of the invalidity ground or become capable of acting freely.[128]

126. T-E. Madell, Det allmänna som avtalspart pp 175 et seq. (1998).
127. See Part I s. 1 L.
128. See s. 1 II.

III. Restitution

289. The provisions on restitution upon termination in sections 64–65 of the Sale of Goods Act are generally considered applicable by analogy to invalid contracts at large also in cases of restitution due to invalidity.

290. When performance rendered under an invalid contract is to be restituted each party may withhold restitution of what it received until the other party renders its restitution and offers security for any damages and interest that the party may be liable to pay (Zug um Zug). Further, all yield falling from the performance shall be restituted and compensation paid for the benefit that the restituting party may have had due to the performance. If payment is to be restituted, interest is payable from the day when the restituting party received the payment.

291. Restitution of physical objects can give rise to questions about a duty to take care of the object. In principle such a duty of care arises as a consequence of invalidity (and termination). Compensation for reasonable care costs is regularly granted.[129]

IV. Damages

292. In addition to restitution of performance under the invalid contract, a party may be liable to pay damages to the other party. Where performance has been made and reversal of the performance is not possible, damages may be awarded in lieu of the value of a restitution. When no performance has been made, the innocent party may claim compensation for the costs for entering into the invalid contract, the so-called reliance interest (Sw: *negativa kontraktsintresset*). In cases of fraud, compensation may also be had for the expectation interest (Sw: *positiva kontraktsintresset*)

129. See ss 72–73 of the Sale of Goods Act.

Chapter 3. The Contents of a Contract

§1. The Different Clauses

I. Ascertaining of Express Terms

293. Express terms of a contract are ascertained with the aid of ordinary semantics and syntactic rules. The ascertainment gives rise to a prima facie understanding of the contract that is presumed to correspond to the common intention of the parties.[130]

II. Implied Terms

294. Obligations may be implied following from the purpose of the agreement, good faith or sheer reasonableness, such as in NJA 2005 p. 142 where a lessor had a *right* to adjust the interest rate to reflect the prevailing market interest rate. He had increased the interest rate along with the increasing market rate. When the market interest rate sank, he was held to have an implicit *obligation* to decrease the applied interest rate; he had to apply the provision in a loyal and consequent manner.

III. Standard Terms and Exemption Clauses

295. Exemption clauses that are deemed to lead to an unreasonable distribution of risks are generally interpreted restrictively. The clause is then considered not to be applicable to the actual situation at hand although the wording of the clause prima facie covers the situation. A restrictive interpretation can in many cases be less explicit and be transformed to an outflow of the *contra proferentem* rule. The view is then frequently that the wording of the exemption clause contravenes the rest of the agreement. The exemption clause is then given a lower priority. Such clauses can also be modified or set aside pursuant to section 36 of the Contracts Act.[131]

IV. Penalty Clauses

296. Liquidated damages clauses (sometimes referred to as penalty clauses Sw: *viteskIausuler*) are common and may serve three functions.

297. Such a clause can serve as an exemption or limitation of liability clause. The injured party may then only invoke a right to a penalty in case of a breach. The right to penalties replaces 'all other remedies' for the breach and typically leads to compensation for only a part of the loss caused by a breach. A liquidated damages

130. See further s. 2 below.
131. See Adlercreutz & Gorton II, pp 116 et seq.

clause may also be seen as a provision for quantified damages. This is often done in order to avoid the difficulties associated with proving the quantum of damages. A liquidated damages clause may also be used to give a disincentive for delays, particularly in construction contracts and contract for works. The right to a penalty for delay is then typically combined with a more or less limited right to compensation for actual loss due to the breach.

298. Penalty clauses in all of these functions are subject to a reasonability test under section 36 of the Contracts Act. Penalty clauses with the aim to punish the party in breach are deemed to be unreasonable per se.[132]

299. In NJA 2010 p. 629 a liquidated damages clause giving the injured party compensation for about 10% of the actual damages was upheld as an exclusive provision about liability for breach. In NJA 2012 p. 579 the question challenged was whether a party should be deemed to be over-compensated when he received penalties for delay from two contractors. This was held not to be the case with the observation that there might be situations when the compensation would be unreasonably large compared to the actual loss so that an adjustment of the clause could be called for.

V. Arbitration Clauses

300. Arbitration clauses in respect of future disputes in consumer contracts are in general invalid; section 6 of the Arbitration Act (1999:116). Arbitration clauses in commercial contracts are susceptible to be set aside or adjusted pursuant to section 36 of the Contracts Act in cases where the arbitration clause has been inserted in standard terms not easily accessible for the weaker party.[133]

§2. Interpretation

I. Introduction

301. The term 'interpretation' is generally used in a wide sense in Swedish legal literature. The term encompasses the objective process of establishing the meaning of the language and expressions used in the contract formation by means of a semantic and logical analysis. Where such analysis is not conclusive, the interpreter resorts to the context which brings a variety of interpretation data into play. The process results in a prima facie interpretation. The term interpretation further includes the elaboration of the prima facie interpretation by the use of subjective elements; such as what the parties actually intended and what they actually realized. This may lead to a revision of the result of the prima facie interpretation. It is debated to what

---

132. See Government Bill (Prop) 1975/76 s. 118 f.
133. See NJA 1936 p. 521 and NJA 1949 p. 609. See however NJA 1980 p. 46.

extent subjective elements should be assessed in the interpretation of standard agreements.[134]

302. Interpretation 'rules' may be applied in order to resolve conflicts between irreconcilable positions or interpretation results. The term in a wider sense further includes construction or gap-filling of incomplete contracts by means of usage or non-mandatory law. A kind of gap-filling is known as individual construction (Sw: *individuell utfyllnad*).[135] The gap-filling activity of the courts can in some circumstances be influenced by a policy, subject to the freedom of contract principle, to use a case before the court to pronounce directives that may influence the behaviour of other actors. NJA 2005 p. 142 is illustrative in the sense that the Supreme Court pronounced that it was incumbent upon the lessor to apply a clause regarding adjustment of interest rate on a loyal and consequent manner. In sum, this means that interpretation in the wide sense refers to an activity that aims at determining the content of an agreement.

II. Intention of the Parties

303. The principle that a contract shall be interpreted according to the common intention of the parties is a corollary of the principle of freedom of contract. In the cases that reach the courts the problem is that such common intention is rarely possible to establish. Therefore, it is presumed that the wording of the agreement (or rather the prima facie interpretation as described in 4.0 above) reflects the common intention.

304. The party who claims that the agreement does not correspond to this interpretation has the burden of proof. The evidence will be evaluated by the court freely without consideration to any rules on parol evidence.[136] The wording of the agreement is however given considerable weight and will consequently usually prevail.

305. In cases when a common intention cannot be established, UPICC Article 4.1(2) states that the contract shall be interpreted according to the meaning that reasonable persons of the same kind as the parties would give to it in the same circumstances. This principle catches the approach used in Swedish law, although the result of the interpretation process is usually not rationalized with the same expression.[137]

III. Interpretation of Statements and Other Conduct

306. The principles laid down in UPICC Article 4.2 on the interpretation of statements and other conduct of a party are harmonized with Swedish law. This also

134. See Adlercreutz II, p. 68 with further references. In NJA 1990 p. 24, the Supreme Court found that the parties had intended to deviate from standard terms referred to.
135. Compare the German concept '*ergänzende Vertragsauslegung*'.
136. Compare however no. 190 *supra*.
137. Compare however CISG Art. 8(3).

follows from CISG Article 8(1). Thus, statements and other conduct by a party shall be understood according to that party's intention if the other party knew or could not have been unaware of the intention.[138] In principle, for a fact (such as a statement or an action) to be of relevance when the intention is to be established, the other party must be aware of the fact at the time of the conclusion of the contract. It is however sufficient to conclude that he – based on an objective evaluation of the situation – *should* have been aware of the fact. Thus, if a party offers 'x' and the other party should have realized that the first party meant to offer 'y', the first party is not bound by 'x'.[139] If the offeree accepts, the offeror may however be bound by 'y' as intended.[140]

307. It has been noted that this relaxation of the awareness-rule from actual awareness to imputed awareness opens up for pragmatism and courts can reach interpretation results that appear as reasonable or otherwise satisfy general public interests and policies. It should be noted that subsequent facts may serve as evidence of intentions and awareness at the time of the agreement, but such facts are not of direct relevance.[141]

IV. Relevant Circumstances

308. The common intention of the parties is the real agreement. The wording of a written contract is the primary source of evidence when the common intention is established in the interpretation process. The contract may make reference to a standard agreement, a specification, drawing or some other document, which is then deemed to be a part of the contract. In Swedish such documents when attached to the contract are usually referred to as enclosures (Sw: *bilagor*) and there is in Swedish no word for making the English semantic distinction between exhibits (documents being a part of a main document) and appendixes (additional reference information). Samples and models may similarly be regarded as a part of the contract when arriving at a prima facie interpretation.[142] An introductory part of a contract is in principle not regarded as a part of the substantive agreement. When the introduction however contains representations of facts made by one party unilaterally, the other party may rely on its accuracy.[143]

309. The wording – or the result of the prima facie interpretation – is presumed to correspond to the common intention. This means that a contract following an acceptance of an offer of 'x' is presumed to regard 'x' unless the offeror can prove that he intended 'y' and that the offeree realized or should have realized this at the

---

138. Compare no. 143 and no. 147 above regarding the subjective element in s. 4 para. 2 and s. 6 para. 2 of the Contracts Act.
139. See s. 32 para. 2 of the Contracts Act.
140. Compare CISG Art. 8 (2) –(3).
141. Adlercreutz & Gorton II, pp 54 et seq.
142. Compare s. 17 of the Sale of Goods Act and CISG Art. 35(2)(c).
143. See NJA 1993 p. 436.

time of the contract formation. The presumption holds even if a party claims that he has not read the wording.

310. The strength of the presumption varies with the clarity of the wording. It seems sufficient that one party's understanding of the agreement has better support of the wording than the other party's understanding in order for the presumption to arise.[144] When the wording contains contradictory provisions, the rule is that individually negotiated provisions prevail over standard terms and precise terms prevail over generally framed terms.[145]

311. Besides the wording, a range of other circumstances may be of relevance for the verification or the falsification of the prima facie interpretation.[146] Practices and usage can supplement an agreement.. The working method used by the Supreme Court in NJA 1990 p. 24 is illustrative: The case regarded the interpretation of an expression 'all works'. The court found that the wording semantically supported the interpretation made by the purchaser (i.e., a presumption was established). The court went on to investigate whether the contract as a whole or branch practice gave reason to understand the expression in a different manner. Upon finding that this was not the case, the court finally tested whether the prima facie interpretation lead to an unreasonable result.

312. What has occurred during preliminary negotiations may shed light on what the parties have intended.[147] In particular the marketing and other representations made before the agreement are of relevance insofar as the representations can be *assumed* to have influenced the buyer.[148,149] Oral preliminaries during an information meeting affected the interpretation of an index clause.

313. The conduct of the parties subsequent to the contract has indirect relevance as evidence regarding what they intended at the time of contracting.[150] This holds also with regard to agreements that require the observance of formal requirements.[151]

314. Subsequent conduct can also be of direct relevance when the conduct amounts to an agreement to modify a concluded contract. The mere fact that a party has applied contractual provisions in a manner generous to the other party (Sw: *kulans*) is generally not sufficient to amount to a contract modification.[152] Questions

144. Compare NJA 1956 p. 209.
145. See Adlercreutz & Gorton II, p. 61.
146. Compare UPICC Art. 4.3.
147. See e.g., NJA 1964 p. 454 and CISG Art. 8(3).
148. See s. 18 of the Sale of Goods Act.
149. See also NJA 1984 p. 280.
150. See e.g., NJA 1946 p. 679 and 1951 p. 645.
151. See NJA 1968 p. 525. Compare also CISG Art. 8(3).
152. See Adlercreutz & Gorton II, pp 101 et seq.

regarding the relevance of subsequent facts often arise in connection with confirmation letters and invoices.[153] An invoice – and presumably terms related to the payment – is presumed to correspond to the agreement unless the receiver protests.[154]

315. The nature and purpose of the contract has been considered in a number of cases.[155] An unclear warranty was deemed to be a warranty for function rather than a warranty for a certain component due to the purpose of the agreement. Similarly, a clear provision can be deemed as inapplicable when it can be concluded from the purpose that the parties did not intended that it should be applied in an atypical situation.[156] A provision requiring a notice period for the purpose of facilitating an employer's planning was not applied when employees terminated the contract and the employer had decided to wind up his business. On the other hand, a narrowly framed provision can be expanded to reflect the assumed purpose.[157]

V. Reference to Contract or Statement as a Whole

316. From what has been said above it can be concluded that Swedish law is congruent with the principle expressed in UPICC Article 4.4, which states that terms and expressions shall be interpreted in light of the whole contract or statement in which they appear.

317. Thus, in NJA 1940 p. 179 the provision on price was relevant when determining the intended scope of sale of real property. In NJA 1990 p. 24, referred to above, the Supreme Court held that a contract should be seen as an integrated totality and that guidance to the interpretation of one provision frequently can be had from other clauses. This approach was followed in NJA 1992 p. 403, regarding the question whether the failure of a distributor to reach agreed minimum sales amounted to a breach of a warranty with damage liability. The court found that a failure to meet the agreed minimum quantities had been explicitly sanctioned by a right for the supplier to terminate the agreement and that this wording would be redundant if it did not exhaustively regulate the remedies available to the supplier. Hence, the supplier could not rely on a generally framed clause regarding breach in another part of the contract. Further, the court checked whether there were reasons to deviate from this preliminary conclusion. The court found that a warranty would have been risky for the distributor to accept and that there was no usage that a failure to meet agreed minimum volumes should lead to damage liability.

153. See no. 313 *supra*.
154. See s. 47 of the Sale of Goods Act.
155. See e.g., NJA 1992 p. 439) and NJA 1998 p. 3.
156. See AD 1981 p. 143.
157. See NJA 1974 p. 463 regarding the scope of a pledge.

VI. All Terms to Be Given Effect

318. There is no clear evidence for the proposition that the principle expressed in UPICC Article 4.5 is upheld in Swedish law. NJA 1992 p. 403 (referred to above) however indicates that there is a preference to interpret contract terms to give them effect rather than to deprive them of effect or regard them as redundant. In this regard it should be noted however that examples of reductive interpretation can be cited, i.e., cases where it could be argued that in fact contract term have been deprived of effect in order to arrive at a reasonable result.

319. In this connection it should also be noted that the limitation of liability clauses and clauses that give one party a unilateral right to determine the contents of parts of an agreement are subject to restrict interpretation.[158] A limitation of liability clause can regard the available remedies particularly the liability for damages (Sw: *påföljdsfriskrivning*) or the responsibility for factual circumstances (Sw: *egenskapsfriskrivning*). In the latter regard, see section 19 of the Sale of Goods Act regarding 'as is' clauses and similar generally framed attempts at limiting the liability for facts. The seller is responsible notwithstanding such a clause if the goods do not conform to the information about them given before the conclusion of the contract, or, he has omitted to inform the buyer about substantial facts regarding the goods or its use in which the seller must have known and the buyer could reasonably have been expected to be informed about, all to the extent that the information can be assumed to have influenced the buyer. Further, the seller is liable if the goods are of a substantially worse quality than the buyer had reason to assume with regard to the price and other circumstances.

VII. Contra Proferentem Rule

320. The *contra proferentem* rule means that contract terms supplied by one party shall be interpreted against that party if the terms are unclear.[159] The rule is accepted in Swedish law with some modifications. In NJA 2006 p. 53 the Supreme Court held that the rule could be applied so that one of two equally reasonable interpretations of an unclear contract provision can prevail. Thus, the *contra proferentem* rule (as well as other mechanistic interpretation rules) is regarded as a last resort.

321. In consumer contracts, unclear non-negotiated contract provisions will be interpreted to the consumer's favour.[160] In consumer contracts, this rule is applied irrespective of whether the other party's interpretation is equally possible or even is more likely to reflect what the common intention was at the time of contracting.

158. See Adlercreutz & Gorton II, pp 116 et seq.
159. See UPICC Art. 4.6.
160. See s. 10 of the Consumer Contract Terms Act.

VIII. Supplying an Omitted Term

322. There may be cases where incomplete contracts cannot be supplemented by non-mandatory rules, either because such rules are lacking or the supplementation appears to be inconsistent with the common intention. In these cases one may resort to objective legal reasoning aiming at the creation of a stop-gap rule which is adapted to the purported purpose of the agreement and reasonability requirements.

323. Swedish law can here be said to correspond to the generally framed principle in UPICC Article 4.8. It should be noted however that the standards of good faith and fair dealing (Article 4.8.2(c)) and reasonability (Article 4.8.2(d)) include an assessment of which party is closer to bear the risk for the gap. This approach can be seen in cases where the gap is an effect of an exchange of irreconcilable declarations of intent (Sw: *dissens*) forming an agreement that is not to be declared invalid. Generally, the risk is allocated to the party who is the closest to blame for the gap. A variety of ways to reason can be seen. Cases have been resolved by the analogous application of section 6 paragraph 2 or section 32 paragraph 1 of the Contracts Act, so that the agreement corresponds to one party's intention if such party has acted in good faith and the other party must have or should have realized that the intentions were irreconcilable insofar as he has remained passive.[161]

161. See Adlercreutz & Gorton II, pp 130 et seq. with further references.

Chapter 4. Privity of Contract

§1. The Rule of Privity of Contract

I. Third Parties and the Contract

324. Contracts entered into between two parties, A and B, often have implications – not seldom negative ones – for third parties. Contractual performance between A and B may cause the spread of air pollution with damaging effect on third parties, it may have negative implications for commercial competition and drive competitors out of business or cause other types of negative so-called externalities for third parties. However, most such negative implications/externalities are not recognized by the legal system as *rights* for the third party. Legally, a third party usually does not have a right to compensation for externalities caused by the performance of a contract between A and B. *Rights* of third parties are, however, protected so, as a general rule, the freedom of contract for A and B does not allow them to enter into a contract which ignores or impinges on the rights of a third party.

325. When used in the following text, the term 'third party' means any person who is outside the contractual relationship between A and B. Furthermore, it does not include persons who in the capacity of employee, agent or in any other capacity representing the principal, act on behalf of the principal with the legal consequence that only the principal (and not the agent, etc.) becomes bound in the contractual relationship. Special mention should be made with regard to what in Swedish law is called a commission agency (Sw: *kommission*). A commission agent is an agent who in the internal relationship, i.e., in the relationship to his principal is an agent (the principal is the owner of the goods which the commission agent sells/buys) but externally in his relationship to the third party is a seller (buyer) in his own name. Where a commission agent has acted for his principal, no privity of contract is constituted between the principal and the third party (except by assignment); the third party may even be unaware of the fact that he deals with an agent (the principal being undisclosed) and that the goods he is buying actually belongs to another, i.e., the principal. No contractual relationship occurs between the third party and the principal in the case of a commission agency sale/purchase; the arrangement is a two-contract relationship. The term commission agent does not seem to be used for this type of arrangement in English law. In English law this arrangement is defined as 'the institution of an agent acting for an undisclosed principal' and the third party and the principal can there enter into a contractual relationship with each other (by the third party's election or the principal's intervention) and, thus, a one-contract relationship (privity of contract) can be established between them.[162]

326. Many commercial contracts are so-called *public contracts* which means that one of the parties to the contract is a public authority and that payment under the contract is to be made by government/public funds. Such contracts are often the

162. See C. Murray, et al., Schmitthoff The Law and Practice of International Trade, pp 770 et seq. (2012).

result of the special procedure of public procurement (Sw: *offentlig upphandling*), a procedure surrounded by extensive regulation which aims at the overall promotion of various societal goals such as free and fair competition, protection against the squandering of public funds and prevention of corruption. Public contracts are governed by the general law of contracts with the limitations imposed by constitutional and statutory provisions and general principles of public law. 'Third parties' to public contracts that have come about as the result of public procurement are the actual and potential competitors/bidders who were not awarded the contract with the public authority. A third party to a contract which has come about as the result of public procurement procedure has a special right to bring a claim against the public entity provided by the public procurement regulation, The Public Procurement Act (2007:1091), see for instance Chapter 16 section 4 about the right for the third party to have the contract reviewed (Sw: *överprövat*) or declared void (Sw: *ogiltigförklarat*) and Chapter 16 section 20 about the third party's right to damages. The status of third parties to a public procurement contract is in many ways special – as a result of a mixture of private and public law – and is left outside of this presentation.

327. According to a fundamental principle in contract law the contract only confers rights and duties to the parties of the contract. It is not legally possible for the parties to impose an obligation on a third party that has not agreed – explicitly or impliedly – to be bound by that obligation. In Nordic law we call this *the subjective limitation of the contract* (Sw: *avtalsverkningarnas subjektiva begränsning*). In English law, where a similar principle applies, it is called *the doctrine of privity of contract*. In French law it is called *the principle of the relative effect of the contract.*

328. The term *privity of contract* is never used in Swedish law as a label for the subjective limitation of the contract. However, since it is an internationally accepted legal term, in this presentation the term *privity of contract* is used also for the Swedish law principle. The former very rigid English institute of *privity* has its own special history, connected with the doctrine of *consideration,* and even if it has acquired a more modern content through the enactment of the special regulation of The Contracts (Rights of Third Parties) Act 1999, it still may contain differences in its application in comparison with other legal systems.[163] In spite of the risk for misunderstanding, the term *privity of contract* is used in this presentation as a label for the Swedish principle of *the subjective limitation of the contract.*

329. The principle according to which the contract only has effects between the parties is not subject to any specific regulation in Sweden. However, the principle as such is recognized as a general principle of contract law (NJA 1997 p. 44). According to the doctrine of *privity of contract*, it is solely the parties who are bound by the contract, who can change the terms of the contract and execute, transfer, etc. the rights and duties which follow from the contract. A contract imposes

163. See J. Cartwright, Contract Law. An Introduction to the English Law of Contract for the Civil Lawyer, Ch. 10 (2007).

liabilities only on the parties and it is only the parties who can sue each other and be sued under the contract.

330. The doctrine of *privity of contract* is not very flexible and does not always meet the efficiency needs of a modern economy where contractual relationships become more and more complex and intertwined in long chains of contracts or networks of contracts. Claims for performance, damages, etc. under a contract often need to be made towards other actors than the other party of the original contract. Construction projects, transport of goods, financial leasing and other contractual arrangements involving multilateral interaction require legal rules, for instance liability rules, which are not limited by the doctrine of *privity* according to which a party to a contract may sue only the other party to the contract. In a construction project, for example, the developer contracts with the general building contractor who in turn contracts with subcontractors. There is no direct contractual relationship between the developer and the subcontractor although the developer usually has a strong interest in the way the subcontractor performs his work. The developer, A, may not sue the sub-contractor, C, on a contractually based claim for damages but if there is not a contractual chain relationship between A and C, A might be able to sue the sub-contractor C in tort for negligence.[164] The problem with the *doctrine of privity* is apparent in, for instance, the typical financial leasing transaction. Such a transaction usually involves three parties, i.e., the supplier, the lessor and the lessee and consists of two separate contracts, i.e., a sales contract between the supplier and the lessor and a financial lease contract between the lessor and lessee. In the normal financial leasing transaction the lessee selects the supplier and specifies the equipment which is to be leased. Thereafter the lessor buys the equipment from the supplier and becomes owner of the equipment which he then leases to the lessee. The lessee pays rentals – including the amortization of the whole or a substantial part of the cost of the equipment – to the lessor under the leasing agreement. The contractual chain in such a transaction is between the supplier and the lessor (a sale) and between the lessor and the lessee (a lease). There is no contractual relationship between the supplier and the lessee. In the case of, for instance, non-conformity of the equipment, the lessee, under the doctrine of privity of contract, does not have the right to direct his claims directly towards the supplier. In Sweden, this problem is usually solved in various ways through standard form contracts. One such way is to establish a so-called third party contract by which the lessee acquires an independent right vis-à-vis the supplier. Another way can be to assign the lessor's right vis-à-vis the supplier to the lessee.[165]

331. Rare exceptions from the *doctrine of privity* exist under Swedish law as the result of special regulation and also as the result of case law. Transportation, especially maritime transportation, of goods often links together a number of different contractual relationships and the Maritime Code (1994:1009) provides for direct claims against the ship's master (Chapter 6, section 11 of the Maritime Code). In a

164. See the reasoning in the Swedish Supreme Court case NJA 2007 p. 758 with reference to NJA 1986 p. 712.
165. See G. Millqvist, Financial Leasing, pp 142 et seq. (1987).

transport of commodities situation, the sold goods often pass through many owners while in transit and here the doctrine of *privity* is difficult to apply. According to the Consumer Sales Act enacted in 1991, a consumer may, in certain cases when the seller is not available to be sued, direct his claim for nonperformance against the seller's seller or another actor at an earlier stage in the supply chain, for instance the producer (section 46).[166] This right for a contract party to make a direct claim against an earlier actor in the supply chain was considered a novelty in Swedish law when it was introduced in 1991.[167]

332. The right for a third party to sue one of the parties to the contract has also, but only rarely, been recognized in case law and in these cases the relationship between the third party and the sued contract party is treated as a non-contractual relationship . In Swedish Supreme Court case NJA 1987 p. 692 a professional consultant, A, was negligent in the issuing of an evaluation certificate regarding the value of a piece of real estate property, a certificate which A issued on the request of B, the owner of the property. The certificate was then used to certify the value of the property when it was used as security for a mortgage to B from a third party, C. When the owner of the property, B, went bankrupt it turned out that the property was not at all worth the amount stated in the certificate issued by A. Although the certificate was issued in the relationship between A and B, the Supreme Court recognized C's right to sue under the contract (the certificate). According to the Supreme Court, a person who issues an evaluation certificate must be aware of the fact that others might come to rely on it, for instance in a sales transaction or a loan transaction; that is, in fact, often the purpose of such a certificate. Thus, A was liable for the damage suffered by C who had – according to the Supreme Court – had a reasonable cause to rely on the certificate when providing B with a loan for which the real estate was used as security. In a later similar case, NJA 2001 p. 878, the evaluation certificate was explicitly limited to only be used 'for the purpose of a dispute settlement', i.e., an arbitration going on. A bank which had provided a mortgage relying on the evaluation certificate was not entitled to compensation from the negligent expert evaluator since the bank ought not to have relied on the certificate due to the explicit limitation of its reach.

333. If a third party – in collusion with one of the contractually bound parties – interferes in an improper way with the contractual relationship between the parties and thereby causes the party to breach the contract with the other party, the third party might be liable for tortious interference and have to pay damages to the other party (NJA 2005 p. 608).

334. The fact that the contract only binds the parties does not mean that third parties are not *legally affected* by the parties' contract. For example, a contract regarding the transfer of property between A and B might have consequences for a creditor, C, who has a lien on the property.

166. See also Consumer Services Act (1985:716) s. 33.
167. See Government Bill 1989/90:89 p. 53.

II. Contract for the Benefit of a Third Party

335. In Swedish law, the freedom of contract principle implies that a party A, can undertake vis-à-vis a party B to benefit a third party and, also, that two parties to a contract can agree that their bilateral contract shall benefit a third party so that, legally, the third party acquires an independent right from the promise or the bilateral agreement. Under Swedish law such an arrangement is called a 'third party contract' (Sw: *tredjemansavtal*) and such a contract sets aside the *principle of privity of contract.* A typical third party contract is an arrangement where A (the stipulator) agrees with B that B (the promisor) shall convey a benefit to the third party C (the beneficiary). Thus, the third party C obtains a beneficiary right to act on a contract between A and B without himself being a party to the primary contract. A third party contract arrangement does not include agency arrangements where the agent acts on behalf of the principal and is not himself a party to the contract. Neither does it include genuine tripartite or multipartite contracts, such as, for instance, joint ventures.

336. In a third party contract the parties confer by express or implied agreement a right on the third party (the beneficiary). The existence and content of the beneficiary's right against the stipulator are determined by the agreement of the parties. Whether a contract is actually a third party contract or not is determined through interpretation of the contract; it must be evident that the parties to the contract have intended that the contract should create an independent right for the third party (NJA 1994 p. 359 and NJA 2005 p. 142). The beneficiary must be identifiable with adequate certainty by the time the contract is entered into but need not be in existence at that time.

337. In one often cited case, a tenant who – in the house where he lived – carried on business which could cause an increased price for the fire insurance for all tenants in the house, took upon himself in his lease agreement with the landlord to pay for the potentially increased cost for fire insurance for all the other tenants in the house. The Supreme Court found this to be a third party contract which gave each one of the other tenants a direct right to have the increased cost for the fire insurance paid by the tenant who had made this agreement with the landlord.[168]

338. Third party contracts have since long been recognized under Swedish law. No general regulation exists about such contracts; the rules have developed through case law. However, statutes about specific types of third party contractually based rights exist, both in the form of mandatory rules and in the form of default rules. There has been a development from purely contract based rules towards legislation for the protection of third parties affected by the primary contract. For instance, there are mandatory rules providing the right to direct claims for the third party

168. NJA 1956 p. 209.

under the insurance contract, see the Insurance Contracts Act (2005:104), Chapter 9. In such a contract the insurance company (the promisor) through a contract with the insured (stipulator) in certain situations, stipulated in the statute, confers an independent right to a third party (the beneficiary). In this case the third party's independent right follows directly from the statute. Another type of contract which conveys rights to third parties are the collective agreements negotiated between unions and employers regulating the rights of employees. Such contracts derive their third party effect from regulation, i.e., the Co-determination Act (1976:580), section 26.

339. In a genuine third party contract there are still only two parties, A and B. The third party C is, as a rule, not considered a party to the contract. In this sense, he does not have an independent right; if A and B decide to change the contract terms, C's right under the contract might be affected or even disappear. Only in the case where C's right explicitly or impliedly has been made irrevocable, can C be sure that his right is fully protected.

A. Conditions of Validity

340. There are no special formal requirements for the contract between the stipulator and the promisor. Regular rules on invalidity apply. If the contract between A and B is void due to, for instance, the fact that A has fraudulently deceived B to enter into a contract to the benefit of C, the contract conveys no rights to C even if C is in good faith.

B. The Right of the Beneficiary

341. The right of the beneficiary is a right conveyed to him directly as a result of the third party contract between A and B; as a right, it never passes via B, the promisor. Until the beneficiary has received what he has been promised under the third party contract his right is dependent on the actions and rights of the parties to the contract. Before performance is due, the third party cannot make any claims vis-à-vis the stipulator or the promisor. If the contract is declared null and void, C's right is also null and void. The same goes for the situation where the contract is modified under section 36 of the Contracts Act due to unreasonableness; if the promisor's obligations are modified, C's rights under the contract are modified to the same extent. If A and B agree to change the contract, C must bear the consequences of such a change. Breach of contract by the promisor does not influence the third party's right. The stipulator has the right to revoke the benefit conferred to the beneficiary under the contract. However, if C has received and accepted a promise from the stipulator that the contract/the stipulation is irrevocable, the parties to the contract are bound by the third party stipulation.

The bankruptcy or death of the stipulator does not, in principle, change the right of the third party under the third party contract.

C. Rights and Duties of the Stipulator, the Promisor and the Third Party

1. The Relationship Stipulator: Promisor

342. As a general rule, the stipulator A has the same rights under the contract as he would have had, had there not been a third party stipulation. He can free B, the promisor, from his obligation to convey the benefit to the third party, in other words he can revoke the stipulation. Changes of the contract which the stipulator is not entitled to do one-sidedly, he can achieve with the consent of B. If the stipulator does not fulfil his obligations under the contract he might be sued by the promisor as in a usual contract relationship.

2. The Relationship Stipulator: Third Party

343. Once performance under the contract is due, the stipulator can no longer escape from his stipulation. If, before performance is due, he has made the stipulation irrevocable by a promise to the third party and the third party has accepted the promise, the stipulator can no longer revoke his stipulation. Before performance is due, the third party cannot claim any right under the contract.

3. The Relationship Promisor: Third Party

344. The third party's right under the contract is a direct claim against the promisor, but his right is dependent on how the parties to the contract, the stipulator and the promisor, change, modify, etc. the contract. If the third party's right has been made irrevocable by the parties to the contract and the third party has agreed to this, his right cannot be altered or taken away from him by the parties.

D. 'Direct Actions'

345. A contract imposes liabilities only on the parties to it and it is only the parties who can sue each other and be sued under the contract (NJA 1997 p. 44). Under Swedish law, this is the general rule and so-called action directe or a direct claim (Sw: *direktkrav*), meaning that the creditor can sue the debtor's debtor directly, is recognized only in exceptional cases. As a general rule, the final creditor cannot sue the debtor's debtor even in the case where it is the debtor's debtor that has broken the contract between the debtor and the debtor's debtor with the consequence that the debtor then also breaches the contract through non-performance, for instance by delivering defective goods, vis-à-vis the creditor. This is a general principle of Swedish law, considered to have its regulatory expression in section 56 of the Commission Agency Act (2009:865). There it is prescribed that the third party receives a claim only vis-à-vis the commission agent (Sw: *kommissionären*) and not vis-à-vis the principal (Sw: *kommittenten*)/the owner of the property which is subject to the commission sales transaction.[169] There are, however, exceptional situations where such direct claims are possible. According to the Consumer Sales Act enacted in 1991, a consumer may, in certain cases when the seller is not available to be sued, and the goods sold are defective, direct his claim for defective performance against the seller's seller or another actor at an earlier stage in the supply chain, for instance the producer.[170] Direct claim gives the creditor a right to 'jump' in the contractual chain.

346. If there is no direct or indirect chain of contracts between the creditor and a subcontractor, the creditor might be entitled on a non-contractual basis to damages in tort directly from the subcontractor if the subcontractor has been negligent and caused a substantial risk for physical damage to persons and property.

§2. Transfer of Contractual Rights

347. The rights a party has based on a contract can under certain circumstances be transferred to a third person. Such transfer is commonly used in commercial contexts, especially with regard to the assignment of debts.

I. General Principles

348. No special regulation regarding the general law of obligations and transfer of contractual rights exists in Sweden. Instead, the regulation regarding promissory notes, the Act on Instruments of Debt (Sw: *lag 1936:81 om skuldebrev*) is, by analogy, used as a basic set of rules for the law of obligations and transfer of contractual rights, particularly the part of the Act which deals with so-called simple notes (Sw: *enkla skuldebrev*).

349. Under the general law of obligations the right to performance under a contract may be assigned to a third party except where otherwise provided by law. With 'assignment' is meant a transfer through contract or other voluntary act from the 'assignor' to the 'assignee' of the contractually based right/claim. It is most frequently a question of the right to the payment of money, either already payable or payable in the future. Also the right to non-monetary performance can be assigned such as the delivery of goods or the rendering of a service. A claim for damages for non-performance under the contract is also transferable. Future debts can be assigned provided they can be identified with sufficient certainty. Rights to the performance of negative obligations, for instance the obligation not to compete within a certain area or within a certain time, are also covered. Rights may not be assigned if the obligation is of such a personal character that performance cannot reasonably be claimed by the assignee. Claims for wages cannot be assigned until they are due.

---

169. See L. Zachariasson, Direktkrav. Om rätt att rikta anspråk mot gäldenärens gäldenär, p. 121 (1999).
170. Section 46. See also s. 31 and the Commission Agency Act (2009: 865) s. 25.

The transfer of a claim/right implies that it leaves the assignor's assets and becomes part of those of the assignee. The definition also covers transfers for security purposes.

350. The most frequently used type of assignment is the assignment of financial claims/debts. Such claims may be assigned in whole or in part. The marketability of claims representing monetary rights is of great importance, both practically and economically in today's society. Suppliers of goods and services often assign their rights to payment from customers to a financing institution, for instance in the form of *factoring*, as a means to finance their business. This means that they sell their receivables (accounts receivable), i.e., their customers' monetary obligations or debts, to a factoring firm in order to receive liquidity. Receivables financing is typically done through assignment, i.e., the transfer of the property right to the receivables which constitute an intangible asset.

351. Claims related to debt evidenced in negotiable documents are regulated in the Act on Instruments of Debt. Where a right to payment embodied in a negotiable instrument is assigned, negotiable instrument law usually gives the holder of the instrument priority over the assignee. The term promissory note means a note/document which embodies a one-sided, written, independent promise to pay a sum of money. Promissory notes can be of three different kinds. They can either be (1) issued to the holder, (2) issued to a named person or his order, or (3) issued to a named person (nominative). Regarding the question of assignment, the first type of note is transferred by delivery, the second type must be endorsed to be legally transferred whereas the third type, the simple note (Sw: *enkelt skuldebrev*) requires more formalities in order to legally transfer to a third party the obligation to pay the debt. The first two types, the negotiable notes (Sw: *löpande skuldebrev*) are intended to be transferred to new creditor(-s) whereas the third type, the simple note, is not intended to be – but may very well be – transferred to a new creditor. The first two types are issued under the assumption that, normally, they will be transferred to new holders. In the stage of transfer, the negotiable notes show their negotiability in that the underlying debt/contractual relationship is separated from the note and the defences that could be made by the debtor against the first holder cannot be made against a new holder. This is the case, for instance, if the note has come about as the result of fraud by the first holder and the note is then transferred to a new *bona fide* holder/creditor, i.e., a creditor who is unaware of the fraud or does not have any particular reason to suspect that the document has come about as a result of fraudulent behaviour of an earlier creditor. In such a case, the objection by the debtor that the promissory note has come about as the result of fraud is not a valid defence against the new holder (Act on Instruments of Debt, section 15).

352. If the negotiable promissory note has been issued to secure payment in a contractual relationship, the debtor may not, against a new *bona fide* holder, make any defences related to the first creditor's non-performance with regard to the underlying contract. Thus, by the transfer of the negotiable note, the new creditor/assignee may acquire a better right than the earlier creditor/assignor. In the case of the simple note, a new creditor cannot acquire a better right than was at the time of assignment held by the earlier creditor/assignor. Defences of invalidity of the promise underlying the promissory note, or that payment has already been made are valid against a new bona fide creditor in the case of transfer of the simple note but not in the case of transfer of the negotiable notes. There are, however, absolute defences available to the debtor in the case of negotiable notes, for instance, (1) forgery, (2) incapacity and (3) duress. When transferring the promissory note to a new creditor the creditor/assignor does not warrant that the debtor has no valid defences. The assignor only warrants that he is the owner of the right and that the debtor is obliged to perform.

353. The rules regarding the assignment of rights embodied in negotiable instruments differ in important respects from regular assignment and, therefore, a deeper investigation into these instruments fall outside the scope of this presentation.

354. Also financial instruments such as bonds and stocks differ in important respects from ordinary rights governed by the law of obligations and, therefore, the transfer of such rights/documents is not included in this presentation.

355. Transfer of rights can also be done through the transfer of other types of documents, called negotiable documents of title. An important such document is the bill of lading (Sw: *konossement*) used in international trade, especially at the carriage of goods by sea. The bill of lading represents the goods in transit, and enables the bearer of the document to dispose of the goods by endorsement and delivery of the bill of lading to a third person. Negotiable bills are normally used in the commodity trade where bills of lading are often purchased and sold in so-called string contracts.[171] The transfer of various documents of title are covered by special rules and are not included in this presentation.

II. Effects of the Assignment

356. As a general rule, the assignment of contractually based claims is effected by the mere agreement between the assignor and the assignee. Thus, the assignment does not require the consent of the debtor. As soon as the assignment takes place, the assignor ceases to be the creditor and the assignee becomes the creditor in relation to the assigned right. The transfer from the assets of the assignor to those of the assignee affects the rights of different third parties. A necessary element for the assignment to have legal effect against the creditor's creditors is the notification to the debtor about the assignment.

357. The debtor is discharged by performing to the assignor so long as the debtor has not received notification (Sw: *denuntiation*) of the assignment from either the assignor or – which is more likely – from the assignee. Once the debtor

171. See Murray, Carole et al., Schmitthoff The Law and Practice of International Trade, p. 319 (2012).

knows or has a reasonable cause to suspect that the assignor is no longer the creditor, he is not discharged by paying the assignor (Act on Instruments of Debt, section 29). In other words, in such a situation payment made to the original creditor will not free the debtor; instead, if he pays to the original creditor he risks to have to pay the same amount also to the new creditor/assignee. The new assignee is not entitled to enforce the claim before the assignment has been notified to the debtor or recognized by him. The debtor may invoke against the new creditor all substantive and procedural defences to the claim based on the assigned right which he could have invoked against the assignor. The same goes for his right to set off.

III. The Transfer as against Third Parties (Other Than the Debtor)

358. Once the ownership of the contractually based right to performance has been transferred and the debtor has been notified about the assignment, the assignor's creditors can no longer seize this claim/asset (Act on Instruments of Debt, section 31). Instead, the creditors of the assignee may seize the claim in question. If all debts belonging to a business are assigned along with the business, the assignee has proprietary protection from the date when the assignment was agreed. Through the assignment, the assignee acquires the same rights as were held by the assignor. The debtor can invoke the same defences against the assignee as he could earlier invoke against the assignor.

359. If the same claim/right is assigned to more than one assignee – something which, normally ought not to happen, but which may occur in practice – preference is given to the earliest assignment. However, if a later assignment is notified to the debtor before notification of the earlier assignment, the assignment first notified to the debtor is given preference, provided the assignee is in good faith, i.e., does not know or ought not to have known about the earlier assignment (Act on Instruments of Debt, section 31).

§3. Transfer of Contractual Obligations and of the Whole Contractual Position

360. Not only rights but also obligations under a contract may be transferred. Such transfer may serve useful economic purposes. Usually the transaction is a transfer of the obligation to pay money, but it can also be a matter of transferring obligations relating to other kinds of performance, such as the provision of services. Also obligations deriving from tort law are transferable. If the debtor wants to be substituted as debtor by assigning his obligations under the contract to a third party, this can be done through a contract and all three of them, i.e., the creditor, the debtor and the third party, have to be in agreement about the assignment. The effect of such a substitution is that the original debtor is discharged.

361. The new debtor may invoke against the creditor the same defences which the original debtor could have invoked against the creditor.

362. In addition to the assignment of claims/rights and to the transfer of obligations under a contract it is also possible to transfer the whole contractual position of a party – both the rights and the obligations – to a third person. In such a case the third party, through substitution, becomes a party to the contractual relationship. Such substitution takes effect only where, as a result of the other party's assent, the first party is discharged.

§4. SUBCONTRACTING

363. A party may use a third party for the performance of the contractual obligations. The contract between the debtor and the third party is then a subcontract to the main contract. Except where the main contract requires a personal performance of the debtor or where subcontracting is prohibited by statutory law or by express contract terms, a third party may be authorized by the debtor to perform the main contract. The creditor may refuse such performance only if it could cause loss or damage to the creditor.

364. The subcontract between the debtor and the third party is independent of the contract between the debtor and the creditor. In other words, there is no contractual relationship between the creditor and the third party, the subcontractor, and, as a rule, the creditor cannot sue the subcontractor but has to direct his claim against his own party to the main contract, the debtor.[172] The third party carrying out the performance often acts on the directions of the debtor. The performance of the subcontractor is usually intended to discharge the debtor vis-à-vis the creditor and due performance by the third party actually discharges the debtor vis-à-vis the creditor.

I. The Liability of the Main Contractor for the Defective Performance of the Subcontractor

365. As a general rule, a party to a contract may entrust the performance to a third party. However, a party who entrusts performance of his obligation under a contract to another person normally remains responsible for this person's performance. In other words, if the subcontractor does not perform, the debtor remains legally bound vis-à-vis the creditor. It is a general principle in Swedish law of obligations that the debtor is answerable vis-à-vis the creditor for non-performance or defective performance of the subcontractor. A seller who engages a third person to help him perform under the contract between the seller and the buyer is liable vis-à-vis the buyer for non-performance or defective performance of that third person.[173] In other words, if the non-performance or the defective performance is a result of the subcontractor's behaviour, the debtor is liable for this non-performance/defective performance as if he had himself caused the non-performance/defective performance. Exceptions from this rule are stipulated in regulation regarding specific types of contracts. Mention could be made of the rule which stipulates that

172. NJA 1997 p. 44 and NJA 2007 p. 758.
173. Sales of Goods Act s. 27, para. 2.

if – in the case of a sale of goods – the parties have agreed that the seller shall deliver the goods to the buyer in another place than the one where the seller is situated, the liability of the seller passes to the buyer at the moment the goods are handed over to an independent carrier.[174] In other words, in such a case the seller is not responsible for negligence of the independent carrier during the transportation of the goods. Only if the seller has been negligent in the selection of the independent carrier (*culpa in eligendo*) is the seller potentially liable vis-à-vis the buyer for damage to the goods during the transportation.

366. In contractual arrangements involving multilateral productive interaction, for instance a construction project, direct claims cannot be made from the contract party to the general building contractor vis-à-vis a subcontractor who is a party in a normal contractual chain; the contract party to the general building contractor has to direct his claim against his party to the main contract, the general building contractor (NJA 2007 p. 758). However, if there is no direct or indirect chain of contracts between the creditor and a subcontractor, the creditor might be entitled on a non-contractual basis to damages in tort if the subcontractor has been negligent and caused a security risk for substantial physical damage to persons and property (NJA 1986 p. 712).

II. The Relationship Employer-Subcontractor

367. Under Swedish law an 'employer' is a party to an employment contract and not just any principal who engages labour in a contract relationship. In other jurisdictions the word employer is used in a broader sense covering also the person who engages self-employed persons, i.e., independent contractors. In order to avoid confusion about the content of the Swedish law, the contractual partner of the main contractor is here called 'the principal' instead of 'employer' in the following text.

368. The principal/the creditor, as a result of the doctrine of *privity of contract*, does not have a direct contractual relationship with a subcontractor engaged by the main contractor/the debtor. Thus, no direct contractual action is available for the principal against the subcontractor and the same is true for the subcontractor vis-à-vis the principal.

369. The principal may, however, in certain situations, have a possibility to sue the subcontractor in tort, see above under 'Direct actions', no. 345.

§5. Oblique Action, the Paulian Action and Direct Actions (Rights and Duties of Third Parties)

370. Under Swedish law the question of third party rights is usually approached as a question of exceptions to the rule of *privity of contract*. The contract between

---

174. Sales of Goods Act s. 7, para. 2.

A and B cannot impose obligations on C, a stranger to the contract; an explicit obligation for C to respect the contract between A and B is not to be found in Swedish law. There are no special contract law principles in Sweden similar to the ones found in France where the contractual situation between A and B generates rights and duties on the part of third parties and where the contract gives rise to a legal situation, a social fact, which everyone must take account of even if they are outside the contract and therefore not a contracting party (the so-called principle of 'opposability' of the contract).[175] This principle, giving substance in French law to the concepts of the *oblique action* and the *paulian action* (as a reminiscence of Roman law) is not recognized under Swedish law. These 'actions' build on the conception that a contract can only produce an effect in as much as it does not result in an infringement or unlawful modification of third party rights. The *paulian action*, for instance, refers to the situation where a debtor A, already contractually obliged to an initial creditor B, enters into a new contract with C which has the effect of compromising A:s performance of his obligation towards B. If C knows that the new contract will cause A to breach his contractual obligation vis-à-vis B, according to the *paulian action*, C commits a delictual fault vis-à-vis B (ibid.) And there exists in Swedish law nothing like the French rule saying that 'a third party to a contract may invoke, on the basis of delictual liability, a contractual failure to the extent that this failure has caused him harm'. (Guiding Principles of European Contract Law p. 83).

371. Rules reminding of the ones just described, if at all existent in Sweden, are to be found in bankruptcy law or/and – only rarely – in tort law. For instance, in the Swedish Supreme Court case NJA 2005 p. 608, a third party who through fraudulent behaviour which was considered extremely unconscionable in collusion with one of the parties to a contract had caused the breach of the contract, was held liable in tort to the other party to the contract. In that case the Supreme Court concluded:

> *According to Swedish law, the point of departure is that a party to a contract that suffers damages as a result of breach has to recover his loss from the other party to the contract. However, this does not mean that, especially in serious cases, a third party that in an extremely unconscionable manner (*Sw: *på ett kvalificerat otillbörligt sätt) interferes with the contractual relationship of others, to the effect that one of the parties to the contract breaches the contract to the detriment of the other party, could not be held liable for damages under Swedish law.*

175. See Guiding Principles of European Contract Law, Société de legislation (2008), at www.legiscompare.fr/Site-web/IMG/pdf/19_Guiding Principles.pdf, p. 81 (visit 28 Oct. 2013).

Chapter 5. The End of the Contract

§1. PERFORMANCE

I. Determination of Quality of Performance

372. Where the quality of the performance is neither fixed by, nor determinable from, the contract a party is bound to render a performance of a quality that meets the reasonable expectations of the other party (insofar as the first party *should* have realized the expectations).[176] In certain contractual relations, or as regards obligations to use best efforts, the quality standard can best be described as lack of negligence.[177] In some contractual relations, the standard of diligence is subject to statutory provisions.[178]

II. Price Determination

373. Where a contract does not fix or make provisions for determining the price, the parties are considered, in the absence of any indication to the contrary to have made reference to the price generally charged at the time of the agreement for such performance in comparable circumstances in the trade concerned or, if no such price is available, to a reasonable price.[179] See also Chapter 13 section 10 paragraph 1 and Chapter 16 section 6 of the Maritime Act (1994:1009). The former provision is not based on the time of the agreement-standard, but looks at the price 'generally charged at the time when the goods were received for transportation'.

374. A related question regards the situation when one party means that there is an agreement on a fixed price and the other means that the price is to be current. The present position in Swedish law – at least in sales and construction contracts – is that the party who claims that the price has been agreed or that there is an agreement on a price calculation formula has the burden of proof.[180] See however section 51 of the Consumer Services Act, which gives a presumption for what the consumer claims to have been agreed about the price in a consumer construction contracts. In NJA 1989 p. 215 regarding the price for book keeping services, the burden of proof that a fixed price had been agreed was placed on the customer with consideration *inter alia* to the difficulties to agree on a fixed price for services of the kind in question.[181] A journalist providing services to a political party assumed that he should be paid for the services. The court found that he had due cause for his

176. See s. 17 para. 3 of the Sale of Goods Act and, as for service contracts, s. 4 of the Consumer Services Act (1985:716) with reference to professional standards (Sw: *fackmässighet*). Cf. UPICC Art. 5.1.6.
177. See e.g., s. 5 of the Commercial Agency Act (1991:351).
178. See e.g., ss 11–19 of the Real Estate Broker Act (1995:400).
179. See s. 45 of the Sale of Goods Act, CISG Art. 55 and s. 36 of the Consumer Services Act (1985:716). Compare UPICC Art. 5.1.7.
180. See NJA 2001 p. 177 (commercial transaction) and 2005 p. 205 (consumer transaction).
181. See in general Hellner & al., pp 41 et seq. Compare also NJA 1969 p. 409.

assumption and that he had not been negligent when not realizing that the other party had assumed that the services were to be provided for free.

III. Contract for an Indefinite Period

375. A contract for an indefinite period may be ended by either party by giving notice to the other party a reasonable time in advance. This principle is seen in Chapter 2 section 24 of the Act on Partnerships (1980:1102). In some cases the notice time is set in statutory law; see section 24 of the Commercial Agency Act and section 33 of the Commission Agency Act.[182] *Cf.* however section 7 of the Act on Protection of Employment Contracts (1976:580), which also requires a valid cause for termination.

376. The main principle that a contract for an indefinite period can be terminated at any time without requirements on the cause can be modified as a result of supplementary interpretation. NJA 1992 p. 439 regarded a settlement agreement in a dispute regarding a trademark and company name dispute. According to the agreement one of the parties were given the right to incorporate a firm dominant in its name. After a time, the other party terminated the agreement maintaining that it was concluded for an indefinite period of time. The Supreme Court found that 'a natural interpretation' of the agreement gave that the parties had agreed that the right to use the name was granted as long as the use otherwise could lead to a dispute between the parties.

IV. Time of Performance

377. A party must perform his obligation at the time fixed by the contract or, when a period of time is fixed or determinable from the contract, within that period unless the other party is to choose the time.[183] If no time is fixed by the contract it will be supplemented.

378. The performance of monetary obligations becomes due on demand.[184] In sales contracts the buyer in principle does not have to pay until the seller provides the goods; *Zug um Zug*.[185] In a work contract, payment is generally considered due when the party providing specific performance has completed its performance.[186,187] A lessor's obligation to pay is due at the end of the lease period. See however the special provision in Chapter 12 section 20 of the Land Code; a tenant is to pay the rent in advance.

182. See also Ch. 12 s. 4 of the Land Code.
183. See UPICC Art. 6.1.1(a) and (b).
184. See s. 5 of the Act on Instruments of Debt.
185. See s. 49 of the Sale of Goods Act and CISG Art. 58.
186. Compare s. 41 of the Act on Consumer Services.
187. See however Ch. 13 s. 10 para. 1 of the Maritime Act (payment for freight is due when the goods are received by the transporter).

379. Specific performance becomes due within a reasonable time after the conclusion of the contract. This principle is confirmed in section 9 of the Sales of Goods Act and CISG Article 33.[188]

380. Swedish law is congruent with the principle that a party must perform its obligations at one time if possible and the circumstances do not indicate otherwise.[189]

V. Computation of Time Set by the Parties

381. When a party unilaterally or the parties by agreement fix a period of time within which an act must be completed, they may stipulate an absolute point of time by setting a date or stipulate a relative point of time, such as within a number of days from an event, e.g., delivery. In the latter case the question may arise as to whether holidays are included. By analogy, the Act (1930:173) on computation of time according to law applies. This means that time set according to week, month or year will elapse on the day that by its name corresponds to the week day from which the computation of time started (i.e., from Wednesday to Wednesday), Time set according to month elapses on the corresponding day from which the computation of time started (i.e., from 5 March to 5 April). In case there is no corresponding day in the following month, the time elapses on the last day of the month (i.e., from 31 March to 30 April). If the time elapses on a Saturday, Sunday, public holiday, Midsummer Eve, Christmas Eve or on New Year's Eve, the time elapses on the first following business day.[190] See also CISG Article 20(2), which is directly applicable to contracts for the international sale of goods. It should be noted that if an action (e.g., a termination) is agreed to take place no later than on a fixed date and this date is a Sunday, the time elapses on that day and not on the following business day.[191]

VI. Partial Performance

382. Swedish law appears to be congruent with the principle set forth in UPICC Article 6.1.3 which states that the obligee may reject an offer by the obligor to perform in part at the time performance is due unless the obligee has no legitimate interest in so doing. Specific exceptions are however to be found in section 34 paragraph 2 of the Cheque Act (1932:131) and section 39 paragraph 2 of the Act on Bills of Exchange (1932:130).[192]

---

188. Compare UPICC Art. 6.1.1(c).
189. See UPICC Art. 6.1.2.
190. See also The Act on Instruments of Debt s. 5.
191. See Rodhe, Obligationsrätt p. 119 et seq [cit Rodhe].
192. See Rodhe, pp 457 et seq.

383. It ought to be noted that the right to reject defective performance in general seems to require that the defect is substantial or the breach otherwise is material.[193]

VII. Order of Performance

384. A general principle regarding the order of performance can hardly be formulated as regards Swedish law. Clearly, the principle set forth in UPICC Article 6.1.4 (1) – a *Zug um Zug* principle – is confirmed in section 49 of the Sale of Goods Act and CISG Article 58, but it does not seem to amount to a general principle. Likewise, the principle set forth in UPICC Article 6.1.4 (2), stating that a party whose performance requires a period of time has to render its performance first, cannot be taken as a general principle in Swedish contract law although it seems to be valid in most service contracts.

VIII. Earlier Performance

385. It seems that a creditor in general has to accept an early performance of a payment obligation unless he has a legitimate interest to refuse acceptance. The same seems to apply in cases of specific performance at least when the performance regards delivery at the creditor's place of business. Even if the creditor would have the right to refuse acceptance of the earlier performance, he may be under an obligation to take care of the deliverables on behalf of the debtor.[194] The creditor is in principle entitled to compensation for costs associated with an acceptance of an early performance or costs for taking care of the deliverables in case of a refused acceptance.[195]

IX. Place of Performance

386. If the place of performance is not determinable from the contract, payment obligations are to be performed at the obligee's place of business. A payment obligation is regarded as a *Bringschuld* in line with a term borrowed from the German legal tradition.[196,197] *Cf.* however UPICC Article 6.1.6(2). In case of a payment by fund transfer or similar payment methods, the place of payment can hardly be determined.

387. A principle for the determination of the place of performance of other obligations can hardly be formulated.[198] The performance of an obligation to deliver goods is however as a general rule to be performed at the obligor's place of

193. See Rodhe, p. 457.
194. See Rodhe, p. 455.
195. Compare UPICC Art. 6.1.5 (3).
196. See s. 3 of the Act on Instruments of Debt.
197. Compare UPICC Art. 6.1.6 (1) (a).
198. See Rodhe, p. 114.

business. Hence, such an obligation is regarded as a *Holschuld*. This is confirmed in section 6 of the Sale of Goods Act and CISG Article 31(c). If the obligee changes its place of business subsequent to the conclusion of the contract, the original place of business will still be the place of performance. This applies both with regard to payment obligations and obligations to deliver.

X. Payment Methods

388. Swedish law seems to be congruent with the principle set forth in UPICC 6.1.7 (1) stating that payment may be made in any form used in the ordinary course of business at the place for payment. The payment method can be considered agreed by subsequent terms set forth in an invoice unless the obligor protests.[199] Where the payment obligation is fulfilled by a transfer of funds, particular problems may arise when the actual time of payment shall be determined. UPICC Article 6.1.8(2) states that the obligor discharges his obligation when the transfer to the obligee's financial institution has become effective. In principle this corresponds to Swedish law. The principle has been elaborated upon in a number of court cases.[200] The present standpoint of Swedish law seems to be that a payment by a transfer of funds is made when the obligor cannot revoke the payment instruction. This point of time coincides with the point of time when the intermediary of the transaction enters the payment into its books. Since this can be done at any time during the day, it is to be presumed that the payment has been made early on the payment day.[201]

XI. Currency

389. Where a monetary obligation is not expressed in a particular currency, payment is to be made in the currency of the place where payment shall be made.[202] If a monetary obligation is expressed in a currency other than the place of payment, it may be paid in the currency of the place for payment or in the currency in which the obligation is expressed according to the choice of the obligor unless the parties have agreed otherwise.[203] Another exception would be that the currency of the place for payment is not convertible.[204] The obligor loses his right to choose if he is in delay.[205] This in principle leads to the acceptance of the principle expressed in UPICC Article 6.1.9(2), i.e., where it is impossible for the obligor to pay in the currency in which the obligation is expressed, the obligee may require payment in the currency of the place for payment.

199. See s. 47 of the Sale of Goods Act.
200. See e.g., NJA 1998 p. 23.
201. See Herre, Svensk rättspraxis: Förmögenhetsrätt 1978–2004, SvJT 2005, p. 549 at p. 679.
202. Compare UPICC Art. 6.1.10.
203. See s. 7 para. 1 of the Act on Instruments of Debt.
204. Compare UPICC Art. 6.1.9.
205. See also Rodhe, pp 35 et seq. and pp 98 et seq.

390. Payment in the currency of the place of payment is to be made according to the applicable exchange rate prevailing there when timely payment is due. If the obligor is in delay the obligee may choose between the exchange rate at the agreed time for payment or the time for the actual payment.[206]

XII. Costs of Performance

391. Swedish law is congruent with the principle expressed in UPICC Article 6.1.11 that each party shall bear the costs of performance of its obligations.

XIII. Imputation of Obligations

392. When an obligor who owes several payment obligations to the same obligee, the obligor may specify at the time of payment the debt to which it intends the payment to be applied to. This follows from an old provision in the original Commercial Code from 1734 (Sw: *Handelsbalken*); see Chapter 9 section 5 of the Commercial Code.[207] The obligor however loses this prerogative if he is in delay, whereupon the obligee may choose how to apply the payment.[208] The obligor cannot choose to apply the payment to an obligation that is not due before applying it to an obligation that has become due. Regarding the requirements on the clarity of the choice of the obligor.[209]

393. Swedish law is not settled as regards default rules for imputations. There is nothing to indicate that Swedish law would not be congruent to UPICC Article 6.1.12(3) giving a preference for the obligation which is first to fall due, then the one for which the obligee has least security, etc.[210]

394. Likewise, it appears that Swedish law is based on the principle expressed in UPPIC Article 6.1.13 stating that the principles in Article 6.1.12 apply with appropriate adaptations to the imputation of non-monetary obligations.[211]

XIV. Application for Public Permission

395. Swedish law relating to obligations to make applications for public permissions is not settled in detail. It can be assumed that the law will be elaborated with due regard to the principles expressed in UPICC Article 6.1.14-6.1.15 and 6.1.17. When permission is neither granted nor refused within an agreed period or within a reasonable time without being due to any fault by a party, UPICC Article 6.1.16(1)

206. See s. 7 para. 2 of the Act on Instruments of Debt.
207. Compare UPICC Art. 6.1.12 (1).
208. Compare UPICC Art. 6.1.12(2).
209. See e.g., NJA 1989 p. 177.
210. Compare BGB s. 366.
211. Compare Rodhe, pp 162 et seq.

entitles either party to terminate the contract. It is questionable whether this principle would be incorporated or whether the situation would be resolved in line with the somewhat different principles under section 23 of the Sale of Goods Act. Performance is not required if there is an impediment that the obligor cannot overcome or it would require efforts that are unreasonable in view of the obligee's interest of obtaining performance. If the impediment ceases within a reasonable time, the obligee may require performance. What is a reasonable time for waiting for the grant of permission and what is a reasonable time to wait for the impediment to disappear may not coincide. In any event it seems that the interest of the obligor would prevail.

§2. Non-performance

I. Non-performance Defined

396. Non-performance is defined as the failure of one party to perform any of its obligations under the contract, including defective and late performance. To use the distinction between obligations to achieve a specific result and obligations of best efforts non-performance occurs as soon as the promised result is not achieved in the former case and as soon as the requirements on diligence are not met in the latter case. The characteristic feature of non-performance is that the obligor can resort to a remedy of any kind.[212]

II. Interference by the Other Party

397. A party may not rely on the non-performance of the other party to the extent that such non-performance was caused by the first party's act or omission or by another event as to which the first party bears the risk.[213] This principle is reflected in sections 22 (regarding delay) and 30 (regarding defects) of the Sale of Goods Act. The provisions would be analogously applicable across the whole field of contract law.

§3. Impossibility, Frustration and Hardship: 'The Unforeseen'

I. Introduction

398. There is no generally accepted catch it all Swedish legal term for what sometimes is referred to as 'hardship'.[214] The terms refer to subsequent unforeseen events that fundamentally alters the equilibrium of the contract whether this is due to increased costs of performance or the diminution of the value of the other party's

212. Compare UPICC Art. 7.1.1. See generally, Rodhe, pp 7 et seq.
213. Compare UPICC Art. 7.1.2.
214. See UPICC Art. 6.2.2–6.2.3.

performance. Swedish law has not incorporated the German way of working with impossibility as a part of a system of the law of obligations, neither the English force majeure based approach. Again, the pragmatic underpinning of Swedish contract law resists any attempts to reduce it down to basic principles. Clearly, unforeseen circumstances, whether occurring before or subsequent to the conclusion of the contract may be regarded in order to modify or terminate obligations under a contract. The tendency in Swedish law has however been to give more relevance to increased performance costs. The law in cases of diminution of the value of the other party's performance – such as when one party's purpose of the contract is frustrated – is meagre. The judicature mostly regards the effect of inflation, which has been dealt with by resort to contract adjustment. In some cases resort has been had to the so-called doctrine of failed assumptions (Sw: *förutsättningsläran*).

II. Modification and Cease of Obligations Due to Unforeseen Circumstances

399. As noted above, the obligation to render specific performance ceases if there is an impediment that the obligor cannot overcome or it would require efforts that are unreasonable in view of the obligee's interest of obtaining performance.[215] There is no distinction made between impediment that existed at the time of the conclusion of the contract or subsequent impediments similar to the one seen e.g., in German law between *ursprungliche* and *nachträgliche Unmöglichkeit*. The provision in section 23 would have analogous application across the whole field of contract law as regards specific performance. The fact that the obligee's right to request performance may cease does not mean that it does not have other remedies. The central remedy in this situation is the obligee's right to claim damages for non-performance.

400. An obligation to pay does not cease. The obligor's liability during the time an impediment exists is set forth in section 7 paragraph 2 of the Act on Instruments of Debt which is inspired by exemption due to force majeure. The liability to pay default interest rate is however strict subject to the rarely used possibility to adjustment pursuant to section 8 of the Interest Rate Act (1975:635).

401. Apart from giving rise to impediments to performance, unforeseen circumstances can render performance unreasonable in other ways. In such cases the contract can be declared void according to the rather esoteric doctrine of failed assumptions which draws on the German scholar Bernhard Windsheid's reasoning in *Die Lehre des römischen Rechts von der Voraussetzung* (1850). An erroneous assumption (Sw: *felaktig förutsättning*) or an assumption that subsequently fails (Sw: *bristande förutsättning*) can lead to voidance if the other party was aware of the assumption and that it was fundamental for the first party's will to conclude the contract and that the risk for the failure of the assumption should reasonably be borne by the other party. The doctrine of failed assumptions is not frequently applied. In NJA 1981 p. 269 the doctrine was applied to a settlement agreement

215. See s. 23 of the Sale of Goods Act.

between a tenant and municipality according to which the tenant abstained from the right of prolongation of a land lease contract due the municipalities' plans to change the use of the land. The plans were later abandoned. The Supreme Court found that the municipality was closer to bear the risk for the failed assumption. In NJA 1985 p. 178 the doctrine was applied when declaring a contract for the delivery of steel to a shipbuilding yard to be void due to the buyer's bankruptcy. The Supreme Court found that the buyer had given the seller an exaggeratedly optimistic view of the buyer's financial ability in a way which reduced the buyer's incentive to make his own assessment of the financial risk. The approach to focus on culpable elements on the side of the other party was reiterated in NJA 1997 p. 5 regarding the sale of a condominium apartment. Here the doctrine was not applied due to the absence of such culpable behaviour.

402. Besides the possibility to declare a contract void according to the doctrine of failed assumptions, changes in circumstances can also result in unreasonableness of continued performance and lead to adjustment according to section 36 of the Contracts Act. This avenue has been used in long-term contractual relationships where inflation has led to a disproportionate balance between the values of each party's performance. NJA 1983 p. 385 regarded a 49 year long land lease contract at a fixed yearly payment with a kind of index mechanism based on the price for wheat. The index mechanism failed to the extent that the lessor could use the land at a remarkably low price. The Supreme Court found that at the time of the agreement (1950) the experience of index clauses was limited. The landowner could therefore not reasonably foresee that the index clause would be insufficient to compensate for the inflation.[216] The case NJA 1994 p. 350 regarded an agreement which exempted a number of house owners from paying waste water fees. The Supreme Court found that later legislation had made similar agreements impossible and that the difference between the exemption from fees and the fees according to the prevailing fee regulations had increased over time. The case contains obiter dicta by the court signals that the application of section 36 should be restricted.

403. Finally, it should be noted that long-term agreements that are concluded for a specified period of time could be cancelled due to important cause (Sw: *viktig grund*).[217] See section 26 paragraph 1 item 2 of the Commercial Agency Act and section 35 paragraph 1 item 2 of the Commission Agency Act.[218] The possibility to cancel seems limited to agreements that require personal performance. An example of due cause for premature cancellation is that an agent without fault falls permanently ill or is injured so that it cannot reasonably be required that he shall continue to perform the contract. An example of a different kind is that requirements on trust fail without being attributable to a party as breach such as the case may be when one party discovers than the other party gives or takes bribes.

216. See however NJA 1979 p. 731.
217. Compare the German concept *wichtiger Grund.*
218. See also Ch. 2 s. 24 para. 3 of the Partnership Act.

§4. Discharge by Agreement

404. An obligee may release its rights by agreement with the obligor as is also stated in UPICC Article 5.1.9(1). A release of rights between a creditor and a third party may however lead to the debtor's loss of right of redress against the third party. The creditor is therefore deemed to be under an obligation not to release such third parties.[219]

405. It is questionable whether Swedish law is congruent with the principle expressed in UPICC Article 5.1.9(2). The matter coincides with the requirements set for a gift to be completed. The requirements vary depending on the property concerned.[220] As regards gratuitous releases of contractual claims, the 'gift' is completed when the debtor is notified.[221] Hence, in this regard Swedish law corresponds to the principle in UPICC Article 5.1.9(2).

§5. Novation

406. The concept of novation is sometimes used to explain how obligations under a contract can come to an end. A novation typically requires that a party releases the other party of his obligations against a promise by the released party to undertake something else. A novation may thus occur after a renegotiation or settlement.[222]

407. A mere prolongation of the contract term or the transfer of rights do not constitute a novation.

408. A novation has in principle three effects. After a novation, the obligee cannot invoke surety or collateral placed by a third party as security for the right performance of the old agreement. In general, prorogation clauses (which require written form) in the old agreement do not apply to the new agreement, whereas arbitration agreements and choice of law provisions may apply to the new agreement insofar as they can be deemed to have been tacitly agreed to apply to the new agreement.

219. See Rodhe, p. 264.
220. See Hellner & al. II.1, pp 283 et seq.
221. See s. 3 para. 3 of the Act on Gifts (1936:83).
222. See generally Rodhe, pp 640 et seq.

Chapter 6. Remedies

§1. General Provisions

409. The general principle is that non-performance gives the entitled party recourse to remedies. The remedies available differ depending on the breach. The remedies in cases of a delay differ from the remedies available in cases of defective performance and other cases of non-performance such as delivery of the wrong goods or delivery at the wrong place.

410. The general policy is that a contract should come to an end after specific performance. In cases of delay, the obligee may terminate if the delay is substantial. The right to damages depends on the applicable prerequisites for liability. In cases of defective performance, the policy is that the obligor should be given an opportunity to rectify the defect or render new performance. The right to terminate is in principle subject to a failure to cure the defect and further requires that the defect is substantial.

§2. Specific Performance

411. Performance of monetary obligations may be required notwithstanding impediments to pay. An impediment to payment does not affect the right to performance, but may lead to a payment delay in which case the party entitled to payment will be compensated by a default interest rate.[223]

412. It should be noted that a seller may not always continue his performance in order to earn the purchase price when a buyer cancels the purchase, unless the cancellation leads to a substantial detriment for the seller. Upon cancellation the seller is entitled to damages corresponding to the accrued costs and the lost profit.[224]

413. As regards performance of non-monetary obligations, Swedish law is in conformity with the general principles expressed in UPICC Article 7.2.2. This is to say that the obligee may require performance, unless performance is impossible, enforcement is unreasonably burdensome or expensive, performance may reasonably be obtained from another source.[225] The right to require specific performance is also limited where performance is of an exclusively personal character. Unlike UPICC Article 7.2.2 the party entitled to performance does not lose the right to require performance unless he makes the requirement within a reasonable time after he has, or ought to have, become aware of the non-performance. Instead, the right is lost if the party lets an unreasonably long time pass before making the requirement.

223. See IX below.
224. See s. 52 of the Sale of Goods Act.
225. Compare s. 23 of the Sale of Goods Act.

§3. Termination

414. The general requirements for a right to terminate a contract under Swedish law in general correspond to the principles set forth in UPICC Articles 7.3.1–7.3.6. Thus, a party may terminate the contract where the failure of the other party to perform an obligation under the contract amounts to a fundamental non-performance. In determining whether a failure to perform an obligation amounts to a fundamental non-performance one considers whether the non-performance substantially deprives the aggrieved party of what it was entitled to expect under the contract (unless the other party did not foresee and could not reasonably have foreseen such result) or whether strict compliance with the obligation which has not been performed is of essence under the contract (such as the case may be e.g., when a Christmas tree is delivered the day after Christmas). Other considerations include whether the non-performance is intentional or reckless. In cases of delay the aggrieved party may also terminate the contract if the other party fails to perform before an additional time for performance has expired (*Nachfrist*).[226]

§4. The Defence of Non-performance by the Other Party

415. Where the parties are to perform simultaneously (Zug um Zug), either party may withhold its performance until the other party tenders its performance and where the parties are to perform consecutively, the party that is to perform later may withhold its performance until the first party has performed.[227]

416. As for specific performance the principle is reflected in section 10 of the Sales of Goods Act and CISG Article 58(1).

417. As for the right to withhold the performance of a payment obligation the principle is reflected in section 42 of the Sale of Goods Act. A buyer may withhold as much of the payment as corresponds to his claims in a case of late delivery or delivery of defective goods. It should be noted that the right to withhold payment here continues after the performance as it covers the buyer's claims due to the breach. The right to withhold payment can in principle be exercised only as far as the payment obligation connects to the other party's obligations under the contract (Sw: *konnexa fordringar*). Payment under one contract cannot be withheld due to a breach of the other party in another contractual relationship. Section 62 of the Sale of Goods Act and CISG Article 72 regulates the right to withhold performance of a payment obligation in view of an anticipatory breach. It is not settled to what extent a party has a right to withhold payment in contracts outside the scope of the Sale of Goods Act, particularly in case of an anticipatory breach. It can be assumed that such a right exists at least in a case of an actual breach and that it can be exercised until the other party performs.[228]

---

226. See s. 25 of the Sale of Goods Act.
227. Compare UPICC Art. 7.1.4. This reflects the concept of *exceptio non adimpleti contractus*.
228. See generally Hellner & al. II, pp 168 et seq.

§5. DAMAGES AND EXEMPTION CLAUSES

I. Introduction

418. The right to contractual damages is regarded as secondary in nature in the sense that damages may be awarded when other remedies – in particular the right to request performance – are not sufficient to repair the consequences of a breach of contract. The main rule is that damage liability requires that the party in breach has acted negligently, but the subjective requirements vary between different kinds of contracts. The applicability of the '*casus mixtus cum culpa*' principle is uncertain in Swedish law.

419. The relation between contractual and non-contractual damages has been and is still subject to scholarly discussion. The Tort Liability Act (1972:207) is applicable to both kinds of damage liability. Statutory provisions and contract law principles then apply to modify the provisions of the Act. It should be noted that liability for pure economic loss according to the Act requires that the loss is due to a crime or that liability follows from statutory provisions or a contract. Notwithstanding this, the Supreme Court has been willing to award compensation for pure economic loss in relations that can be characterized as quasi-contractual.[229] Damages for *culpa in contrahendo* can appear in two forms. When *culpa in contrahendo* is invoked in cases when a contract has been formed, such as when one party has negligently provided incorrect information on which the other party has relied (or negligently omitted to give information), the damage liability is characterized as contractual. Typically these situations are dealt with as a matter of liability for the quality of the performance. When *culpa in contrahendo* is invoked in situations where the negligence had as a result that an agreement was not formed, the liability is in principle non-contractual, which means that the aggrieved party is entitled to compensation for costs that have become unnecessary, but not compensation for benefits that would have arisen if a contract had been formed. The position is similar, in situations where one party has caused an agreement to be invalid. It is however to be assumed that the aggrieved party is entitled to full compensation in cases of fraud.[230]

II. Liability for Negligence

420. Swedish law does not conform to the principle expressed in UPICC Article 7.4.1. Rather the starting point is that non-performance gives the aggrieved party a right to damages insofar as he can prove that the other party (or a third party engaged to perform) caused the breach by acting negligently. This starting point is subject to modifications. The following description does not purport to be exhaustive for all modifications that are upheld.

229. See e.g., NJA 1987 p. 692, 1996 p. 700 and 2001 p. 878.
230. See generally, Hellner & al., Speciell avtalsrätt II.2, pp 200 et seq.

421. A party is strictly liable for his guarantees, i.e., representations regarding existing facts or warranties regarding future facts. Whether a statement amounts to a guarantee with strict liability or merely amounts to information with liability for negligence will be determined as a matter of contract interpretation.[231] The Sales of Goods Act section 40 paragraph 3 bars imputed guarantees as it is required that the guarantee must be explicit (Sw: *särskilt ... utfäst*). In the sale of real estate, it follows from Chapter 4 section 19 of the Land Code that guarantees may be imputed (Sw: *anses utfäst*). It can be assumed that the Sale of Goods Act section 40 paragraph 3 expresses a generally accepted contractual principle. A guarantee *stricto sensu* should be distinguished from seller guarantees or warranties in individual agreements or standard terms, the function of which may be to create a presumption for the fact that a defect existed when title to the goods passed to the buyer or clarify that the seller is responsible for the functionality and which also may impose limitations on the seller's damage liability.

422. The scope of the damage liability for non-performance to some extent relates to the application of other remedies. The liability may be characterized as stricter in particular when an agreement is terminated in response to the other party's wrongful termination or rescission. In agency contracts the party in breach is awarded the possibility to prove that he did not cause the termination by negligence.[232]

423. The scope of the damage liability for non-performance also depends on whether the non-performance amounts to a delay or amounts to defective performance. A seller of real property is subject to strict liability for a delay to leave the sold property and for any failure to complete the sales documents.[233]

424. According to section 27 of the Sale of Goods Act, the seller is liable for direct losses, unless he is excused under circumstances corresponding to CISG Article 79; i.e., delay due to an unforeseeable and unavoidable impediment beyond his control. The liability for indirect losses requires that the buyer can prove that the seller is negligent. The distinction between the liability for direct and indirect loss is particular to sales transactions under the Act and does not apply to international sales under the CISG. What is to be regarded as a direct respective an indirect loss is not clearly defined but indicated in section 67 of the Act. On a general note it can be said that direct losses are foreseeable in the sense that they would occur as a result of the breach independently of the aggrieved party's individual circumstances where as indirect losses are harder to foresee since they depend on circumstances particular to the aggrieved party.

425. In agency contracts, a delay is presumed to be due to negligence, but the party in breach has the opportunity to prove lack of negligence. See section 34 of

231. See NJA 1976 p. 678.
232. See *infra* no. 425.
233. See Ch. 4 ss 13–14 of the Land Code.

the Commercial Agency Act and section 43 of the Commission Agency Act. Likewise it is accepted that the same liability regime applies to lease contracts.

426. As regards defective performance the following modifications should be noted. According to section 41 the Sale of Goods Act, CISG Article 41 and Chapter 4 section 21 of the Land Code, the seller is strictly liable for his ability to deliver goods that are free from third party claims (Sw: *rättsliga fel*). The provisions have analogous applicability. A seller of real property also seems to be strictly liable in cases where the quality of the property is negatively affected by decisions or ordinances issued by public authorities (Sw: *rådighetsfel*). Regarding other defects – in the absence of an explicit or implied guarantee – the seller is liable in case of negligence.

427. Strict liability with the exception of force majeure is seen in transportation law along with a presumption for negligence. Damage liability can also be excluded as in the case of nautical errors.[234]

428. The above brief description should be enough to illustrate the lack of an ambition in Swedish law to put the rules on damage liability for non-performance into a system of overreaching principles. Rather the law has developed under the influence of historical traditions and current practical needs to protect both parties' legitimate interests in a pragmatic fashion.[235]

III. Full Compensation

429. Swedish law corresponds to the principle set forth in UPICC Article 7.4.2. Hence, the aggrieved party is in principle entitled to full compensation for harm sustained as a result of non-performance unless the party in breach has a limited liability. This principle is reflected in section 67 paragraph 1 of the Sale of Goods Act and CISG Article 74. The principle is however subject to modification. Statutory provisions may lead to adjustment of the liability. According to section 70 of the Sale of Goods Act, the damage liability can be adjusted if the liability is unreasonable with regard to the possibilities to foresee and prevent the harm (i.e., with regard to circumstances subsequent to the agreement). A general provision on adjustment of damage liability with regard to the economic circumstances of the liable party appears in Chapter 6 section 2 of the Tort Liability Act. The provision has limited practical importance when it comes to damages for non-performance.

430. There has to be a causal link between the non-performance and the loss. The aggrieved party generally has to prove causality. In some cases the requirements on the proof may be relaxed so that it is sufficient that the aggrieved party makes it predominantly likely that there is causality. Besides causality, the

234. See Ch. 13 s. 26 of the Maritime Act.
235. See generally Hellner & al., II.2, pp 209 et seq with further references.

aggrieved party in principle also has to prove that the loss was a foreseeable consequence of the non-performance.

431. The harm includes both loss which the aggrieved party has suffered and any gain of which he has been deprived, taking into account any gain to the aggrieved party resulting from his avoidance of costs or harm; *compensation lucri cum damno.*[236]

432. The harm may be non-pecuniary and includes e.g., physical suffering or emotional distress. Such personal damage and damages due to loss of property is assessed pursuant to Chapter 5 of the Tort Liability Act. However, the compensation for loss of property does in principle not include affection value.

IV. Certainty of Harm

433. Compensation is due only for harm that is established with a reasonable degree of certainty.[237] This principle relates to procedural requirements regarding proof. In principle the harm has to be proven. Modifications of this principle occur. In NJA 1991 p. 625 regarding the liability for negligent tax advice, the Supreme Court held that it was not possible to determine what the loss ultimately would be since it depended on future and uncertain events such as changes and amendments in tax law. The harm was deemed to correspond to the expenses caused by the negligent tax advice unless the advisor managed to make it probable that the ultimate harm would be less.

434. It may be difficult to prove the harm – or proof would lead to considerable difficulties. In such cases, the aggrieved party is relieved from the requirement to prove the harm, which instead is assessed discretionarily by the court pursuant to Chapter 35 section 5 of the Procedural Code.

435. Swedish law does not explicitly regard 'loss of a chance' as harm, but it can be no doubt that similar harm can be compensated. Swedish law does however not recognize the principle laid down in UPICC Article 7.4.3(2). Although not regarding non-performance NJA 2000 p. 712. The case regarded a company that had not been given the opportunity to participate in public procurement in breach of the Public Procurement Act. The court found that it was sufficient that the company proved that it was probable that the contract was lost due to the breach in order for the company to get compensation for harm beyond the mere unnecessary costs. The compensation should correspond to the character of the breach, the costs and to a reasonably assessed loss of profit.

236. See NJA 1990 p. 705.
237. Compare UPICC Art. 7.4.3(1).

V. Foreseeability of Harm

436. Swedish law diverges from the principle set forth in UPICC Article 7.4.4 stating that the non-performing party is liable only for harm which it foresaw or could reasonably have foreseen at the time of the conclusion of the contract as being likely to result from the non-performance. The principle can be said to be based on the well known English case Hadley v. Baxendale. Swedish law builds on a slightly different approach usually referred to as the theory of adequacy (Sw: *adekvansläran*), the gist of which is that there must be sufficiently close connection between the breach and the harm from an objective point of view. The practical difference between the two approaches may be small, but the difference should be noted. The principle set forth in UPICC Article 7.4.4 is however recognized in international sales of goods.[238]

437. The theory of adequacy is modified through *perpetuation obligationis*, which means that a party who is liable for delay is also responsible for unforeseeable consequences of the delay. Further modifications follow from the policy that only harm that can be deemed to be worthy of protection due to the purpose of the agreement will be compensated. This is often referred to as '*normskyddsläran*' and is akin to the German theory regarding the *Vertragszweck* as a principle for limiting the contractual damage liability.

438. Two examples from the judicature can be given to illustrate how Swedish courts can reason.

NJA 1991 p. 217 regarded a two and a half hour delay by a bank to pay out money which was deposited by a customer. The customer had bought a house on an auction and immediately managed to resell the house at a profit. The latter transaction was however not possible to pursue due to the delay (the prospective buyer walked away). The customer claimed compensation for loss of profit and for loan costs that had not arisen had the house been sold. The Supreme Court found that the harm must be foreseeable and that a bank had reason to take into consideration that even a small delay could lead to losses of the kind in question. It was also found that the customer had explained to the bank why a timely payment was of the essence. Similarly, in NJA 1998 p. 893 a credit institute was in delay with the processing of an application for a house loan. The delay led to additional financing costs for the applicant and to the fact that the loan when it was granted carried a higher interest rate due to market fluctuations. Compensation for the harm was awarded. The Supreme Court found that the market for interest rate was volatile and that it was self-evident that a delay amounted to a risk that the applicant could be exposed to a higher interest rate when the loan finally was granted. It was not to be regarded as an unexpected or improbable consequence of the delay. Compensation for the harm including the additional financing cost was awarded.

238. See CISG Art. 74.

VI. Proof of Harm in Case of Replacement Transaction or by Means of Current Price

439. Where the aggrieved party has terminated the contract and has made a replacement transaction within a reasonable time and in a reasonable manner it may recover the difference between the contract price and the price of the replacement transaction as well as damages for any further harm.[239] This is also referred to as grand damage computation (Sw: *stor skadeståndsberäkning*). Proof of harm by current price in case where there is no replacement transaction can be furnished pursuant to section 69 of the Sale of Goods Act, CISG Article 76.[240]

VII. Harm Due in Part to Aggrieved Party

440. Swedish law corresponds to the principle set forth in UPICC Article 7.4.7. That is to say that where the harm is due in part to an act or omission of the aggrieved party or to another event for which that party bears the risk, the amount of damage is reduced to the extent that these factors have contributed to the harm, having regard to the conduct of each of the parties.[241] See also Chapter 6 section 6 paragraph 2 of the Tort Liability Act.

VIII. Mitigation of Harm

441. Swedish law is congruent with the principle expressed in UPICC Article 7.4.8, i.e., that the non-performing party is not liable for harm to the extent that the harm could have been reduced by the aggrieved party by reasonable steps. This principle is expressed in section 70 paragraph 1 of the Sale of Goods Act and CISG Article 77 and is analogously applied across the whole field of contract law as an expression of a general contractual principle.

442. Since in agreements regarding the sale of goods under the Sale of Goods Act, a distinction between the liability for direct versus indirect loss is made, it should be noted that costs resulting from attempts at reducing indirect losses are to be regarded as a direct loss.[242] Consequently, the liability to pay compensation for such harm is strict.[243]

IX. Interest for Failure to Pay Money or Damages

443. The right to claim interest for failure to pay is regulated in the Interest Rate Act (1975:635).

239. See s. 68 of the Sale of Goods Act, CISG Art. 74. Compare UPICC Art. 7.4.5.
240. Compare UPICC Art. 7.4.6. See generally Hellner & al. II.2, p. 226.
241. See NJA 1997 p. 127.
242. See s. 67 para. 3.
243. Compare UPICC Art. 7.4. 8(2).

444. If the maturity date is set by the agreement interest rate accrues from the maturity date. The interest rate amounts to the reference rate set at any time by the National Swedish Bank plus 8%. Thus, the claim for interest rate in case of payment delays can be said to include a penal element in the sense that it does not take account of the fact that the creditor might not have had access to such interest rate in the alternative that payment had been made timely.[244]

445. In cases where the maturity date is not set in advance, such as the case usually is when a party is liable to pay damages for non-performance, the interest rate starts to accrue thirty days after the day when the aggrieved party claimed compensation (not necessarily specifying the amount) and has provided the facts upon which the claim is based.[245] See however UPICC Article 7.4.10 (which states that interest accrues as from the time of the non-performance).

446. The aggrieved party is entitled to damages above the interest if the non-payment has caused additional harm.[246]

447. Claims for compounded interest rate are not subject to compensation under the Interest Rate Act.

448. It should be noted that in cases of re-payment of sums after a termination or in similar situations of restitution of sums paid, the interest rate corresponds to the reference rate plus 2% during the time between payment and the maturity date for the claim for restitution.[247]

X. Manner of Monetary Redress

449. Damages are usually to be paid in a lump sum. In principle a court may however also order the party in breach to pay damages in instalments where the nature of the harm makes this appropriate.[248] Such arrangements are mostly used to compensate the future loss of income in personal injury cases.[249] Section 5 contains provisions for adjustment of the instalments due to materially changed circumstances.

XI. Currency in Which to Assess Damages

450. It is doubtful whether UPICC Article 7.4.2 reflects the position of Swedish law. The article states that damages are to be assessed in the currency in which the monetary obligation was expressed or in the currency in which the harm was

244. See ss 3 and 6 of the Interest Rate Act.
245. See s. 4 para. 3 of the Interest Rate Act.
246. Compare UPPIC Art. 7.4.9(3).
247. See s. 2 para. 2 of the Interest Rate Act.
248. Compare UPICC Art. 7.4.11.
249. See Ch. 5 s. 4 of the Tort Liability Act.

suffered, whichever is more appropriate. The choice is left to the aggrieved party. According to section 7 of the Act on Instruments of Debt (1936:81) the debtor is given the choice. The provision is considered to be of analogous applicability.[250]

XII. Agreed Payment for Non-performance

451. Clauses regarding payment in case of non-performance can limit or expand the liability that follows the supplementary rules and principles described above. Clauses that purport to restrict the liability are subject to restrictive interpretation.

452. A clause can exclude damage liability altogether and leave the aggrieved party to pursue other remedies. Exclusions of the liability for gross negligence or wilful misconduct are deemed to be invalid.[251]

453. More common are clauses that replace the right to damages with the right to receive a specific amount. In cases of delay such sums are usually referred to as a penalty (Sw: *vite*). In case of defective performance such sums are often also referred to as quantified or liquidated damages.[252]

454. In commercial contracts it is very common that the parties exclude liability for indirect loss except in cases of gross negligence or wilful misconduct. Such clauses are in principle to be upheld irrespective of the actual harm. In cases where the clause would lead to a clearly unreasonable result, it can be assumed that the clause can be adjusted under section 36 of the Contracts Act although there are no known examples in the judicature.[253]

§6. Limitation of Actions

455. The basic statutory provisions on prescription (Sw. *preskription*) are found in the Act on Prescription (1981:130). Prescription regards obligations to pay. Thus there is no prescription of claims based on the law of property.

456. The basic limitation period is ten years, although consumer payment obligations have a limitation period of three years (section 2 of the Act on Prescription). This basic principle is modified in case one of several jointly liable debtors has paid a debt and wishes to recover payment from the co-debtors. In such case the period of limitation does not occur prior to one year after the payment of the joint debt.

250. See Rodhe, p. 35.
251. See however Hellner & al. p. 242.
252. Sw: *beloppsbestämt skadestånd.*
253. Compare UPICC Art. 7.4.13.

457. The period of limitation is interrupted if the debtor in any way recognizes his debt, e.g., by a part payment or payment of interest or if the debtor receives a claim or notice regarding the existence of the debt. When the period of limitation is interrupted, a new limitation period of ten years starts to run.

458. A debt subject to prescription may be used to set off a counterclaim (section 2 of the Act on Prescription). It is not possible to agree on a longer period of limitation. The parties can however agree on a shorter period.

459. Besides the basic rules on prescription in the Act on Prescription there are specific prescription rules in statutory provisions that apply to certain contract types. This is not the place to mention all of these rules. As an example section 32 paragraph 2 of the Sale of Goods Act can be mentioned. Thus, if the buyer does not give notice that the goods are defect within two years after receiving the goods, he cannot invoke the defect (unless otherwise follows from a guarantee). The buyer may see his claim based on the defect fall due to prescription even earlier if he does not give notice within a reasonable period of time after having detected the defect (section 32 paragraph 1 of the Sale of Goods Act). It is noteworthy that the seller (debtor) cannot invoke prescription under section 32 if he has acted grossly negligent or acted in an immoral way; section 32 paragraph 1 of the Sale of Goods Act.

Part II. Specific Contracts

Chapter 1. Agency

§1. Regulation Regarding Agency and Other Intermediaries

460. The main rules on agency in general are found in the Contracts Act (1915:218). Under the Act, an agent is a person who has the authority to bind the principal and a third party in a contract without himself being bound by that same contract. Thus, a contract can be made either by the parties themselves or through an agent acting as an intermediary on behalf of a party, the principal. When there is an agent involved in the making of a contract there are three persons acting, namely, the principal, the agent and the third party. If the agent is properly authorized, the contract in question is between the principal and the third party. An agent with the proper authority who makes a contract with a third party on behalf of his principal is merely an intermediary and the contract will bind the principal and the third party but not the agent. In other words, the agent (Sw: *fullmäktig*) never acts in its own name. It must be noticeable for the third party that the agent acts on behalf of somebody else, although it is not necessary for the agent to reveal the identity of the person on whose behalf he is acting, the principal may remain 'undisclosed'. If it is unclear whether the agent acts on his own behalf or on behalf of somebody else, the presumption is that the agent acts on his own behalf.

461. The Contracts Act entered into force in 1916 and, as for agency, some of the regulation has become outdated. The development of the law on agency has mainly been shaped by the courts, but scholarly work has also been quite instrumental for today's understanding of agency in Swedish law (amongst others, Grönfors, K., Ställningsfullmakt och bulvanskap, 1964).

462. Thus, under Swedish law, an 'agent' means a person who acts in the name of the principal.

463. If the agent acts in his own name on behalf of the principal, under Swedish law he is not a mere 'agent' but is then a *commission agent* (Sw: *kommissionär*) with a different legal status, see the Commission Agency Act (2009:865). There is also a distinction made between an agent and intermediaries who act on behalf of a legal person as a result of special regulation, for instance as chief executive officer (CEO) of a private company limited by shares whose authority follows from the regulation in the Company Act (2005:551).

464. Intermediaries whose authority has been bestowed upon them by regulation or by a public or judicial authority, such as commission agents and self-employed commercial agents (Sw: *handelsagenter*) are dealt with separately.[254]

§2. AGENCY UNDER THE CONTRACTS ACT

I. Various Ways to Establish Agency/Mandate

465. Agency covered by the Contracts Act can be established in various ways, for instance through a notice addressed directly to a third party whereby the principal grants agency to the agent (section 13), through a grant of agency which has been published by the principal in the press or otherwise publicly announced (section 14), or – which is probably the most frequently used – through a written document given to the agent to be held by him and presented to third parties (section 16). These grants of agency are all so-called independent agencies; they are noticeable for third parties. If a grant of agency is based solely on a communication by the principal to the agent (section 18) this is seen as an independent agency (not noticeable for a third person). If a third person relies on such an agency he takes a risk as to whether the agent is appropriately authorized by the principal. If the agent acts outside his authority in a transaction, the principal may afterwards ratify the transaction and thereby become bound by it.

466. A special form of agency is the one that follows from occupying a certain position in the service of another (the principal) according to section 10, paragraph 2. If a person who, as employee in the service of another party or otherwise as a result of an agreement with another party, occupies a position which, according to law or custom, confers certain authority to act on behalf of the other party (the principal), that person shall be deemed to be authorized to perform such legal acts (on behalf of the principal) as fall within the scope of such authority. This form of authority, called 'position agency'/'position authority' (Sw: *ställningsfullmakt*) is of utmost importance. In Common Law this form of agency seems to come close to what is called 'apparent authority' but the concepts are defined somewhat differently. Under common law apparent authority (also called ostensible authority) 'is a form of estoppel: if the principal, by words or conduct, indicates that a person has the authority to act on his behalf, and the third party contracts with the agent on that basis, the principal is estopped from denying the agent's authority even if, in fact, the agent was unauthorized'.[255]

467. The Contracts Act regulates the external relationship between the principal and the third party and not, in principle, the internal relationship between the agent and the principal. The Act mainly deals with the various ways in which authority can be bestowed upon and taken away from an agent and how and when an act by the agent is binding /not binding for the principal.

254. See Commercial Agency Act (1991:351) and *infra* ss 3 and 4.
255. See Beale et al., Contract – Cases & Materials, pp 1128 et seq. (2008).

468. In general, 'agency' is established through a legal act by which the principal grants authority to the agent to act on behalf of the principal. If the agent acts within the authority bestowed upon him by the principal and enters into a contract with a third party, the effect of the authority is that the principal immediately and unconditionally becomes bound by the contract with regard to both obligations and rights as if he had himself entered into it. The contract is between the principal and the third party and the agent is not in any way affected by the contract. There are only two prerequisites: that the act is within the boundaries of the authority and mandate given to the agent and that the agent acts in the principal's name on the principal's behalf.

469. In principle, there are no formal requirements as to how an authority of agency shall be formulated. There are no formal requirements, except in the case of transactions regarding real estate. Since there is a formal requirement when it comes to transferring real estate property rights, i.e., the contract must be in writing, there is also a requirement in the Contracts Act with regard to agency; the authority for the agent must be in writing and also clarify which is the relevant property.[256]

II. Agency as a Result of a Certain Position

470. When a person, as a result of an employment contract with the principal 'or otherwise as the result of an agreement with another party', occupies a position with which, according to law or custom, follows authority to act on behalf of the employer or 'the other party', such a person enjoys 'position agency' (section 10 paragraph 2). Employees often have the authority to act on behalf of the principal. However, the authority is limited to what follows from 'law or custom'. The difficult question is how to identify authority that follows from 'custom'. What is 'customary' to do in a certain position in an organization, for instance a company? This question has caused considerable litigation in the courts throughout the years. What is customary must be decided objectively, i.e., it is not the perception of the individual third party that counts but, instead, what normally, in society at large, would be the perception of the authority that follows from a certain position ('… authorized to perform such legal acts as fall within the scope of such authority'). For instance, a salesperson in a department store has the authority to sell the merchandise in his/her department by entering into sales contracts with customers on behalf of the principal (the department store) but does not normally have the authority to settle a dispute with a customer regarding a sales transaction (NJA 1990p. 591). The decisive factor is the well founded reliance of the third party. The prerequisite 'well founded' implies that it is in accordance with custom for the employee in that particular position to be considered to have authority of a certain scope.

471. Position agency is considered to only cover routine issues; agents usually do not have the authority, as a result of their mere position, to enter into more unusual transactions on the principal's behalf. The employer/principal cannot limit

256. Section 27 para. 2, first sentence.

or in any way influence this type of agency by giving instructions; the authority follows from what is normally considered to be the task of a person in the particular position in question, for instance a bank clerk, a sales manager, a janitor, etc. If the employer/principal wants to terminate the authority, he/she has to remove the employee from the position in question.

472. In the Swedish courts there appears to be a tendency to be pragmatic and not so formal in the determination of which positions do and do not confer authority upon the employee and with regard to how far-reaching the scope of such authority ought to be. In scholarly writings, this has caused the development of labels such as 'tolerance agency' and 'combination agency'. Tolerance agency (Sw: *toleransfullmakt*) has been considered to exist in cases where the employer has been passive and tolerated the fact that the employee acted outside the scope of his formal position agency. Combination agency (Sw: *kombinationsfullmakt*) might exist when a number of facts in the particular case are recognized as legally relevant and, combined together, considered to constitute authority, not always corresponding fully to the requirements of the formal position agency under section 10 paragraph 2 of the Contracts Act.

III. The Difference between Authority and Mandate

473. An important distinction is made between the agent's authority and the agent's mandate. This distinction is an expression of the difference between, on the one hand, the independent juridical act through which authority is conferred to the agent (which can also take the form of an express declaration directly to the third party), and, on the other hand, the contractual relationship between the principal and the agent. It is the difference between what the agent may do in accordance with the internal relationship existing between him and the principal, and what he can do in the external relationship with the third party, i.e., his power to bind the principal vis-à-vis the third party. If the principal has given the agent authority to act, for instance in a written document, but has also given the agent oral instructions which limit the agent's scope of action but without telling the outside world about this restriction (the mandate), the agent is obliged to obey these instructions and act only within his mandate. However, if the agent enters into a contract on the principal's behalf and disregards the restrictions, the principal may still be bound vis-à-vis the third party. This will be case in the situation where the third party did not realize, or ought not to have realized, that the agent acted outside his mandate. Accordingly, the third party is considered to have acted in good faith. In such a case, the principal is bound by the contract, as long as the agent has acted within the boundaries of the authority and the third party did not realize – or ought not to have realized – that the agent acted outside his mandate (section 11, paragraph 1).

474. In the Swedish legislative history, the legal act conferring authority is seen as an expression of the will of the principal directed towards the third party, through which the principal takes responsibility of the consequences following from the legal acts performed by the intermediary on the principal's behalf. This will-theory based conception of agency is not so predominant today; instead, Swedish law has developed towards a more pragmatic view of the institution of agency. Today, in many cases, agency is considered to exist also in circumstances where there has not been an express legal act by the principal conferring authority to the agent. Instead of focusing on the intention of the principal, Swedish law places more emphasis on how the situation is perceived from the outside (the reliance principle). Instead of investigating the intention of the principal, the courts find the well founded reliance of a third party being a more important factor when they determine whether in a certain situation a person should be considered to be an agent acting on the behalf of the principal. This means that agency can come about through implicit behaviour by the principal. The decisive principle behind the agency law today is the need for protection of third parties' good faith for the efficient functioning of economic transactions (NJA 2013 p. 659).

IV. Termination of Agency

475. The authority of the agent can be revoked at any time and it is revoked in the same way as it was created. Thus, an express authority, for instance in the form of a written document, is revoked when the principal repossesses the document from the agent.

476. If the principal wants to take away the position authority from an agent the only way to do this is to remove the agent from the position in question (section 15).

V. Ratification. Principal Becoming Bound by Passivity

477. It is important to clarify that the principal can always 'heal' the agent's lack of authority by confirming that he, the principal, accepts the contract (ratification). If the principal does not explicitly confirm the contract, he might nevertheless become bound if he has at earlier occasions not reacted disapprovingly on the agent's acting without authority, but instead acted as if he had accepted the situation. The principal can become bound by his passivity in combination with behaviour showing that he has accepted the contract, for instance, by paying bills generated from the contract. In such a case, the principal's earlier tolerance of the agent's acting outside the scope of authority, becomes a legal fact that constitutes authority for the agent in similar cases where the agent acts outside the scope of his original authority.

VI. Passive Authority

478. An agent who has authority to act on behalf of the principal also has what is called a 'passive authority', i.e., the right to act on behalf of the principal in legal acts against the principal, section 26.

479. This means, amongst other things, that the intermediary has a right to collect money, intended for the principal, for instance the third party's payment of a bill to the principal.

VII. Agent Acting Outside His Authority

480. Under Swedish law the agent is never part of the contract, not even when he exceeds his authority. However, if he acts without authority (*'falsus procurator'*), the agent might be liable vis-a-vis the third party under section 25 which deals with the relationship between the agent and the third party. Swedish law is here in accordance with UPICC Article 2.2.6(1) and (2). If the agent acts outside his authority the principal is not bound by the contract. In that case the third party might be entitled to damages from the agent.

481. The agent has the burden of proof regarding his agency status and he bears a strict liability under section 25. The damages shall amount to the expectation interest, which means that, economically, the third party shall be put in as good a position as it would have been in had the contract been valid. However, the right to damages for the third party depends on whether the third party was in good faith regarding the agent's lack of authority (section 25 paragraph 2).

482. In other words, if the third party is in bad faith with regard to the agent's lack of authority, i.e., if the third party, when entering the contract, actually knew or ought to have known, if he had considered the question further, that the agent lacked authority, then the agent is not liable vis-à-vis the third party.

483. There is an old, still applicable rule in the Swedish Commercial Code (Sw: *Handelsbalken*), Chapter 18, section 3, which – in the case when the agent has acted outside the terms of the grant of authority – grants the third party compensation also from the principal in spite of the fact that there is no valid contract between them. The rule can arguably be said to build on the principle of unjust enrichment (Sw: *obehörig vinst*). The principal may have to compensate the third party for his performance under the (invalid) contract to the extent that the performance has provided value or utility for the principal.

§3. Commission Agency

484. A frequently used agency arrangement is the commission agency. An agent bound by a commission agency contract (Sw: *kommissionär*) with his principal (Sw: *kommittent*) sells or buys goods/chattels or negotiable instruments/securities on behalf of his principal but in his own name. Under a commission arrangement the agent does not bare the risk of having to pay for the goods which he cannot sell and the principal does not have to take the risk of goods placed in the possession of the agent, belonging to the principal, being included in the agent's bankruptcy estate. The sales/purchase contract is between the commission agent and the third party and the third party can claim performance only from the agent (not from the principal). However, the ownership of the goods sold/bought is transferred directly from the principal to the third party and never passes through the agent. The agent is entitled to payment in the form of commission for the transaction. If property belonging to the principal is in the possession of the agent and the agent goes bankrupt, the principal has the right to remove the property.

485. The commission agency relationship is regulated in the Commission Agency Act (Sw: *Kommissionslag 2009:865*). If the principal is a consumer, for instance a private person selling securities through a bank acting as commission agent, the Act is mandatory in the sense that if the agreement between the parties is less favourable for the consumer than are the provisions of the Act, the Act shall apply. If the parties are merchants there is freedom of contract unless the provisions of the Act specifically prescribe differently. Such is, for instance, the case with provisions regarding the agent's right to commission and severance pay and with regard to the agent's obligation to act in the best interest of the principal. The agent is obliged to follow the instructions of the principal, provide the principal with a reasonable amount of information and always notify the principal about the agreements entered into with third parties on behalf of the principal and submit monies received from third parties on behalf of the principal.

486. When the commission contract expires or is terminated, the agent is entitled to severance pay if he has provided the principal with new customers or substantially increased the trade with existing customers and the principal will have a significant benefit from this and if severance pay seems reasonable with regard to the circumstances, particularly considering the loss of commission for the agent from the agreements entered into with the new or existing customers.

487. In case of non-performance by either the agent or the principal, the suffering party may have the right to recover damages. If one of the parties turns bankrupt, the other party has a right to compensation for the damage this caused him.

§4. Self-Employed Commercial Agents

488. A commercial agent is a person (legal or physical) who in the course of his business has agreed with another, the principal, to independently and continuously promote the sale or purchase of goods by soliciting offers or entering into sales contracts on behalf of and in the name of the principal and who performs this activity on a self-employed and commercial basis as an independent contractor (Sw: *självständig uppdragstagare*). Swedish commercial agency law is found in The Commercial Agency Act (1991:351) which reflects the EEC Council Directive of 18 December 1986 on the coordination of the laws of the Member States relating to self-employed commercial agents (86/653/EEC). The Directive covers the internal relationship between the commercial agent and the principal. If there is no provision in the Commercial Agency Act to the contrary, the rules of the Act are default and can be set aside by agreement between the parties, by practice which the parties have established between themselves and by commercial usage or other customs (section 2).

489. The commercial agent is a middleman/an intermediary acting on behalf of and in the name of the principal. The relationship between the agent and the principal is based on a contract. There is no requirement that the agreement has to be in writing but if either party demands it, it should be in writing (section 4). Standard terms are common.

490. In performing his activities a commercial agent must look after his principal's interests and act dutifully and in good faith (section 5). In particular a commercial agent must make proper efforts to negotiate and, where appropriate, conclude the transactions he is instructed to take care of and communicate to his principal offers which have been received and agreements which have been concluded for the performance of the agency contract. The agent also has to comply with the reasonable instructions given by his principal.

491. Furthermore, the principal must act dutifully and in good faith and provide his agent with the necessary documentation relating to the goods concerned. He must also provide the agent with the necessary information for the performance of the agency contract and, without unreasonable delay, inform the agent about the acceptance or the non-acceptance of an offer which the agent has delivered to him or that an agreement which the agent has solicited has not been performed. The principal shall, without unreasonable delay, notify the agent once he anticipates that the volume of commercial transactions will be significantly lower than that which the commercial agent could reasonably have expected (section 7).

492. Since the commercial agent is not an employee but an independent contractor there are special rules in the Act providing the agent with commission on commercial transactions concluded during the period covered by the agency contract, as well as commission on commercial transactions concluded after the agency contract has been terminated (sections 8–10). Usually the agent is also entitled to severance pay when the contract expires (section 28). If a party to the contract does not perform properly under the contract and thereby causes damage to the other party, the suffering party is entitled to damages (section 34).

§5. Brokers

493. A broker is an independent intermediary/middleman whose task is to introduce two parties to each other or to negotiate contracts on behalf of the principal but without any authority to bind the principal. In other words, a broker is not an agent unless he has been granted authority to act as agent. As a rule, the broker is entitled to payment for his work only in the case where the parties reach an agreement. A broker does not bear any economic risk arising from the transaction.

494. No general regulation in relation to brokers exists in Sweden. However, there is special legislation with regard to special types of brokers, such as The Real Estate Broker Act (2011:666) and the Insurance Mediation Act (2005:405). The latter builds on the EU Directive 2002/92/EU and covers not only insurance brokers but also insurance agents. The special legislation about brokers has as a main goal to provide consumer protection; it requires brokers to register and puts them under special inspection by the governmental authorities. Such brokers are also required to adhere to certain standards with regard to competence, to a duty of care (Sw: *god fastighetsmäklarsed*) and to at all times work in the best interest of the consumer/client. The Real Estate Broker Act imposes on the real estate broker, a responsibility in its capacity as a physical person and requires the broker to take both the buyer's and the seller's interest into consideration, regardless of whom the principal of the broker is. However, when it comes to the economic interest, the broker is obliged – in applying its duty of care (Sw: *god fastighetsmäklarsed*) – to particularly consider the interest of the principal (section 8).

495. As a rule, the broker is remunerated in the form of a commission. His right to commission occurs when there is a deal.

§6. Distributors

496. Distributors (Sw:*återförsäljare*) are not middlemen/agents/intermediaries but act as independent contractors on their own behalf. There is no special legislation regarding distributors in Sweden so freedom of contract prevails. However, the rules pertaining to commercial agents can be used by analogy with regard to distributors (NJA 2009 p. 672 where the Supreme Court also referred to the Draft Common Frame of Reference IV.E. -2:302 and found that, even if the parties had not agreed on a notice period for the termination of the sole distributorship contract, the distributor was entitled to a notice period of three months, i.e., three months' severance pay).

497. Distributors have agreements with the other party for whom they are working, so-called distributorship contracts, under which they have taken upon themselves to – often under a certain period of time and in a certain area – distribute/sell a certain amount of the other party's goods which they then purchase and sell independently. They carry the whole economic risk, but, on the other hand, also determine the price themselves and receive the whole profit from the transaction with the third party.

Chapter 2. Bailment

498. Bailment means the transfer of possession (but not ownership or any other property right) of movable property/chattel from one person (the bailor) to another person (the bailee). Under Common Law this is usually not seen as a contract since there is no consideration. Under Swedish law the transaction is seen as a contract (Sw: *deposition*) whereby the bailee receives (possession of) the movable property from the bailor with a duty to keep it, take care of it and return it in kind. A bailment is basically a contract to take care of and exercise good care of another person's property. It can be gratuitous, as is often the case between private persons, or onerous. Bailment is considered to be a so-called real contract, i.e., it becomes binding upon performance (when the chattle is delivered to the bailee). There are old rules in the Commercial Code of 1734 prescribing that the bailee ought to care for the movable property as if it were his own; if it is lost or injured due to the bailee's negligence he is obliged to give full compensation to the bailor (Chapter 12 section 2 of the Commercial Code). If the chattle is damaged during the bailment, the burden of proof is reversed, i.e., there is a presumption for the bailee's liability which means that in order to avoid liability the bailee has to prove that the damage was not the result of its negligence.

499. Regarding the parties' obligations vis-à-vis each other, distinction should be made between contracts between private parties, on the one hand, and commercial contracts, on the other. If the bailor is a consumer and the bailee is a merchant, there are mandatory rules in the Consumer Services Act (1985:716) for the protection of the interest of the bailor.

500. A simple example of bailment is leaving one's clothes in a restaurant in custody of the person who is there to take care of the guests' clothes.

501. The special rules found in some jurisdictions whereby innkeepers liable as 'bailees of necessity' for the destruction, deterioration and taking away of objects brought to the hotel by a traveller who stays there, do not exist in Sweden. Here, regular contract rules and liability rules apply.

502. Under Swedish law bailment is a contract with property law implications. If the bailor becomes bankrupt while he has possession of the bailee's goods through a bailment contract, the bailee – in order to get possession of his goods – has to prove that he has the right of possession (usually as the owner) of the goods in question.

Chapter 3. Aleatory Contracts

§1. Gaming and Betting

503. Swedish law is not altogether clear with regard to claims based on contracts including gaming and betting. Earlier it was held that such contracts were void (pacta turpia) and not enforceable, i.e., the courts would not admit claims. However, if such a debt was paid, it could not be recovered. Today, the courts have admitted claims referring to gaming and betting and the pactum turpe rules are not very often applied to contracts regarding gaming and betting.[257]

257. See also no. 280 above.

Chapter 4. Sale of Goods

504. The Sale of Goods Act (1990:931) contains non-mandatory provisions that are applicable to all sales transactions. The act is based on the 1980 Convention on the International Sale of Goods. Articles 1-13 and 25-88 were adopted by the act on International Sale of Goods (1987:822). Later Sweden has also adopted the provisions on contract formation in Articles 14–24 by the parliamentary act 2011:852.

505. Although based on the convention, the Sale of Goods Act contains a number of provisions that differ from the convention. First, the Sale of Goods Act has a wider area of application that the convention. The Act applies not only to the sale of goods, but also to sale of intangible personal property, such as shares, debt instruments, electricity and intellectual property rights. In the preparatory works of the Sale of Goods Act it was noted that the provisions of the Act might need to be adapted to the specific kind of property sold and to *lex specialis*, such as section 9 of the Act on Instruments of Debt (1936:81) which in general exempts the seller of a debt instrument from liability for the quality of the transferred debt instrument, i.e., the debtors ability to pay.

506. It should further be noted that the Sale of Goods Act makes a distinction between a party's liability for direct and indirect losses. The liability for direct loss (losses that follow directly from the breach and are foreseeable as a typical consequence of the breach) is in principle strict unless exemption under a provision corresponding to Article 79 of the Convention can be invoked. For losses that are idiosyncratic to the injured party or are otherwise hard to foresee, liability requires either that the injured party can show that the other party acted negligently or that the other party (in case of defects) has issued a warranty. The distinction was introduced at a late stage in the preparatory process and is said to have been inspired by the fact that most Swedish commercial standard contracts used the distinction to limit the risk for liability for losses that are hard to foresee. The distinction should be understood against the background that Article 74 of the Convention has no counterpart in the Sale of Goods Act, which instead is based on the principles on foreseeability of harm (Sw: *adekvansläran*) as developed in tort. These principles of foreseeability can be regarded as stricter that the principles behind the Convention Article 74.

507. Other noteworthy differences between Swedish national and international sales law include section 18 of the Sale of Goods Act which imposes on the seller a liability for statements about the goods made by him or anyone acting on his behalf (if the seller should have known about the statements) in the marketing of the goods. There is also a provision in section 19 about sales of goods 'as is'. An 'as is' clause does not exempt the seller from all liability for the quality of the goods. Thus, the goods must still conform to the seller's statements about the goods (when the statements can be assumed to have influenced the buyer's will to make the agreement). The seller is also liable for an omission to inform the buyer about material properties of the goods (as far as known by the seller). The seller is also liable if the goods sold are in a substantially worse condition than the buyer with regard to the price and other conditions could reasonably assume. All auction sales are deemed to be made 'as is'. With regard to remedies, it should be noted that according to section 54, the seller's right to terminate is lost once the goods have been handed over to the buyer, unless the seller has contracted to maintain the termination right (Sw: *återtagandeförbehåll* or *hävningsförbehåll*).

508. Consumers enjoy certain mandatory rights pursuant to the Act (1990:932) on Consumer Sales and pursuant to the Act on Distance Agreements and Other Agreements outside Shop Areas (Sw: *Lag 2005:59 om distansavtal och avtal utanför affärslokaler).* These acts have recently been adapted to implement the EU Directive 2011/83/EU (the Consumer Directive).

Chapter 5. Hire of Work & Skills, Building Contracts

§1. The General Law

509. Contracts regarding the hire of work and skill are service contracts (Sw: *tjänsteavtal*), as opposed to contracts where property is involved which is the case, for instance, with sales contracts. A service contract regarding the hire of work and skill is a contract through which one party, for instance a customer, a client, a patient, a real estate owner who wants to have his house painted, or any other physical or legal entity, here called the principal, entrusts the execution of a definite work to another, the service provider, here called the independent contractor, who carries out the service independently, i.e., without being an employee of or an agent for the principal. Contracts regarding the hire of work and skill constitute a certain category of service contracts. In this presentation, they are simply called service contracts, although this concept, when used more generally, also covers a great number of other types of services, such as insurance.

510. If a contract is a mixed contract, i.e., a contract containing, for instance, both the transfer of property and a service, for instance a contract about both purchase and installation of a machine, one part of the contract might be treated as a sales contract while the other part is considered to be a service contract (Hellner et al. II: 1, p. 92). However, the main rule is that a mixed contract should be defined from the point of view of the dominant content of the contract (Sale of Goods Act section 2, paragraph 2, see also Supreme Court case NJA 2001 p. 138). If the service part is dominant over the sales part of the contract, the whole contract is regarded as a service contract. Contracts for the supply of goods to be manufactured are defined as sales contracts unless the party who orders the goods undertakes to supply a substantial part of the material needed for the manufacture of the goods in question (Sale of Goods Act, section 2, CISG Article 3). If such is the case, the whole contract is considered to be a service contract.

511. The law regarding service contracts makes a distinction between material services (Sw: *materiella tjänster*) and immaterial/intellectual services (Sw: *immateriella tjänster*). A material service can aim at the production of a certain material result, for instance the repair of a car or the delivery of goods. An immaterial service can aim at, for example, providing legal service by a lawyer to a client. In the case of the material service, the service provider shall provide the agreed result. In the case of the immaterial service contract, the provider of the service does not produce a specific result but shall perform the service with the care and skill which a reasonable service provider would exercise under the circumstances. Both types of services shall be performed in conformity with the statutory rules and professional standards applicable to the service. As a general rule, the service provider shall follow the instructions of the principal. A service contract mostly contains a duty of care for the service provider.

512. No special legislation exists in Sweden for service contracts as such. As a point of departure, general rules of contract law and the law of obligations apply.

This means that, in general, principles such as the freedom of contract and of good faith and fair dealing apply and that there are no specific requirements with regard to form. However, various pieces of legislation exist with regard to specific service contracts, particularly within consumer protection law, often the result of EU directives, for instance the Consumer Services Act (1985:716), the Consumer Credit Act (1992:830) and the Package Travel Act (1992:1672). Important legislation regarding service contracts between commercial partners exist in the form of various legislative acts on contracts for the carriage of persons and goods, often building on international conventions. Even if such transport contracts are basically service contracts, they are usually treated separately within the area of transport law and, therefore, they are not included in this presentation.

513. With general legislation lacking, it is difficult to pinpoint which, if any, general rules apply to service contracts. The contract terms, the type of contract in question, analogy to legislation in related areas and general principles of law are sources and instruments used in the finding of the law applicable to service contracts not covered by any specific legislation. As a general rule, liability for the service provider requires negligence. Materials used by the service provider under a material service contract have to be of good quality and fit for the purpose. However, if the service provider in a material service contract also furnishes the material and the property perishes before being delivered, the loss is on the service provider, unless the principal was in delay with regard to receiving the delivery of the property. If, on the other hand, the service provider in a material service contract only furnishes his work and the property perishes, he is liable only for his negligence. Service contracts, material as well as immaterial, imply a duty to perform in accordance with the agreement, with professional standards and custom.

514. The Consumer Services Act is the only more general regulation that exists regarding service contracts related to physical things. The extent to which this legislation could be applied by analogy to other types of service contracts, for instance commercial service contracts, is, however, debated (see Hellner et al., II: 1, p. 90). The Consumer Services Act does not apply to all types of consumer contracts. Only contracts regarding the performance of work on a movable thing (however, not on a live animal), work performed on real estate and the storage of a movable thing (however not of a live animal) are covered by the Act (section 1). Contracts regarding health services are, for instance, not covered. However, the principles of the Act regarding the question when payment is due have been applied by analogy to a contract regarding dental treatment (Supreme Court case NJA 2011 p. 600). The Act does not cover the manufacturing of movable things, the instalment or other work which a seller performs for the fulfilment of a contract regarding the sale of a movable thing (the whole contract is then seen as a consumer sale, covered by the Consumer Sales Act), nor the work which is performed to remedy the lack of conformity by repair of sold goods (also in this situation the Consumer Sales Act applies). In sum, the question regarding which rules apply to service contracts not subject to any specific regulation is difficult to answer in a clarifying way. Solving the legal problems by way of analogy and by referring to general principles of law is common within this area of law. The pieces of legislation most frequently used by analogy and considered to express general principles of private law, are the Consumer Services Act (1985:716) with regard to material service contracts, and The Commission Agency Act (2009:865) regarding immaterial service contracts, a relationship where the service provider has the role of trustee (Sw: *syssloman*), see Government Bill 2008/09:88, p. 22.

515. The Consumer Services Act prescribes that the merchant, in a contract with a consumer covered by the Act, shall perform the service with professional skill (Sw: *fackmässigt*) and that he, with due care, shall act in the interest of the consumer and consult with the consumer to the extent this is needed and possible (section 4). In a commercial service contract relationship, if nothing else has been agreed, the same rule applies by analogy (Hellner et al, II: 1, p. 100).

516. If there is no agreement with regard to the price for the service, according to the Consumer Services Act section 36, the consumer shall pay a reasonable price taking into account the type, the scope and the performance of the service. In the process of finding the reasonable price, the normal (Sw: *gängse*) price or the normal way of calculating the price for equivalent services at the time of the entering into the contract should be considered. Other circumstances (Sw: *omständigheterna i övrigt*) may also be taken into account. This rule also applies to commercial service contracts by analogy (also by analogy from the Sale of Goods Act section 45).

517. When a service is not performed according to the contract and, thus, there is a breach of contract, the remedies can be one of the following or a combination of them, depending on the circumstances and on the type of breach: (1) a right to require performance (specific performance)/right to payment, (2) a right to withhold payment/right to keep the repaired goods until payment is made, (3) a right to price reduction, (4) a right to terminate the contract without notice and (5) a right to damages. With regard to the consequences of breach of contract, there is a difference between consumer contracts and commercial contracts with stronger protection for the consumer.[258]

518. Immaterial service contracts do not have to do with physical things but, instead, are contracts about intellectual/professional services. Such services are the type of services provided by lawyers, auditors, doctors, banks, etc. There is no general legislation covering professional service contracts. Therefore, the Commission Agency Act (2009:865) which is considered to express general principles of private law regarding independent contractors (Sw: *uppdragstagare*) who are also trustees (Sw: *sysslomän*), is often applied by analogy to immaterial service contracts more generally. Section 4 and section 6 of the Commission Agency Act prescribe that the commission agent shall take into consideration the interest of the principal and that the agent has a duty of care vis-à-vis the principal which makes the agent a trustee ('syssloman') of the principal in their internal relationship. If the service provider is not clearly a trustee, for instance a doctor vis-à-vis the patient or a teacher vis-à-vis

258. See, for instance, Hellner et al., II, :1, p. 116.

the student, the obligations of the service provider is less clear, but, generally speaking, similar rules are considered to apply.[259]

519. Special regulation exists with regard to certain immaterial service contracts and a few examples of such legislation shall be given here. The legislation is often mandatory to the advantage of the typically weaker party who can be, for instance, a franchisee or a bank customer seeking financial advice. Thus, as an example, the Act on the Duty of a Franchisor to Provide Information (2006:484) puts on the franchisor a rather extensive, mandatory duty to inform the franchisee before the franchise agreement is concluded. The Real Estate Broker Act (2011:666) clarifies that the role of a real estate broker is to act in the interest of both the seller and the buyer in the real estate transaction and that the broker is under a duty of good faith and fair dealing in accordance with 'good practice' in the real estate broker profession (Sw: *god fastighetsmäklarsed*). The Act on Providing Financial Advice to Consumers (2003:862) requires, among other things, of the service provider, often a bank or another financial institution, to ensure that the person who gives advice to a consumer to invest in financial instruments has enough competence for the task and the service provider has a duty of care to act in the consumer's interest and to provide his financial advice in accordance with the standard of good faith and fair dealing as this is understood as 'good practice' in the finance sector (Sw: *god rådgivningssed*).

§2. Building Contracts

520. A very important type of service contract is the building contract, i.e., a contract about the construction or repair of a building or other real estate (Sw: *entreprenadavtal*). Such a contract regulates the hire by the principal of an independent contractor's work for the purpose of producing a material result in the form of a building or other real estate construction work such as repair or installation. The transfer of the constructed property from the independent constructor to the principal is, normally, also part of the contract. In Sweden there is no general legislation covering the construction of buildings or the development of building projects (similar to, for instance, the Belgian Breyne Act of 1971, as amended in 1993). Therefore, as a starting point, general contract law and law of obligations apply. However, there exists regulation for the purpose of consumer protection. If the building is a one family or a two family residential dwelling and the principal is a consumer, the Consumer Services Act applies, see sections 51–62, 'Special Provisions About the Construction of Small Houses' (Sw: *småhusentreprenad*). This regulation is mandatory to the advantage of the consumer which means that provisions that are more favourable for the consumer than the regulation, may apply. Under this regulation, if no written contract exists, the consumer's statement about what has been agreed with regard to the scope of the work, the price, the time for payment and the time when the work should be completed, shall be taken for good. There are also rules about how final inspection of the construction work should be

259. Bengtsson, Bertil, Särskilda avtalstyper I, 1971, p. 172.

performed, about the presumption of liability for the constructor for defects appearing within two years after the final inspection/completion of the work and other provisions which imply a better protection for the consumer than is provided by the general law of obligations which would otherwise apply.

521. No legislation regarding building contracts between commercial actors exist in Sweden. However, such work is usually carried out under a standard form contract called AB 04. When the special consumer protection rules just mentioned or the special standard form contract AB 04 do not apply, a building contract is not covered by any special regulation. In such a case general contract law and law of obligations apply and to what extent other regulation, for instance the general Sale of Goods Act, could be applied by analogy, is debated. Not even the widely used AB 04 is considered to express usages or customs that could be generally applied by analogy.

522. The standard form contract AB 04 has a long history and has been updated throughout the years. It is a so-called agreed document which means that it is a standard contract negotiated and concluded between established professional actors on both sides (in this case also with the participation of public bodies with authority in the building/construction industry). AB 04 is a highly regarded, widely used document in the construction industry. AB 04 applies when the parties engaged in a construction project have agreed on its application. Since many actors are usually involved in a construction project and several different contracts apply, AB 04 regulates the hierarchy of the different contracts and – if there are conflicting rules between the different contracts – it also explains how the documents should be interpreted in relation to each other. AB 04 contains detailed provisions with regard to the parties' rights and obligations during the construction project. It covers projects where the price is fixed as well as projects carried out on an open account basis (Sw: *löpande räkning*). Important provisions are found in AB 04 with regard to the principal's right to have amendments and additional work performed under the contract. There are provisions in AB 04 about how the parties should cooperate, about payment, inspection, liability for delay, fault and other types of breach of contract and other items that might occur under the period of construction and with the construction when it is finished. Under AB 04 the independent contractor is liable for defects for a period of ten years and provides a guarantee for two years from the acceptance (Sw: *godkännande*) of the construction regarding the material (unless a subcontractor has provided a longer guarantee for particular material in which case the contractor is liable during the same period) and for five years regarding the work performed. If a fundamental defect (Sw: *väsentligt fel*) caused by the contractor's negligence, appears after the guarantee periods, the contractor is liable for such a defect. The contracting parties are responsible for acts performed by their employees or sub-contractors. The right to terminate the building contract without notice (Sw: *hävning*) is, of course, problematic and is regulated in great detail in AB 04.

Chapter 6. Lease, Commercial and Agricultural Leases

523. Swedish law on lease contract law is basically contained in the Land Code (1970:944) (Sw: *jordabalken*). The provisions are far too detailed and technical to be suited for a presentation down to the exact nature of the rights and obligations that may arise out of a lease contract. The following is an attempt to present only the structure and general nature of the kinds of contracts concerned.

524. General provisions on the right to use real property based on agreements are given in Chapter 7 of the Land Code. The provisions cover a variety of forms for use such as forestry, fishing and hunting rights and the right to electricity. The provisions are mostly of a property law nature or otherwise quite general. It is noteworthy that an agreed prolongation of such agreements are regarded as a novation pursuant to Chapter 7 section 7. Cf no.406 above. The basic provisions are elaborated in Chapter 8 on lease contracts (Sw: *arrende*) in general. The provisions in Chapter 8 regard *inter alia* the forms for termination and the effects of impediments to the enjoyment of the lease. More detailed provisions applicable to the different forms of leases are given in subsequent chapters. Chapter 9 regards agricultural leases (Sw: *jordbruksarrende*), Chapter 10 regards leases of land for living or housing purposes (Sw: *bostadsarrende*) and Chapter 11 regards leases of land for the purpose of conducting business activities (Sw: *lägenhetsarrende*). The provisions are quite detailed. If any general principles are to be pointed out it can be said that many provisions regard the property law aspects of lease contracts and that the freedom of contract has been limited with a view to protect the lessee who is typically regarded as the weaker party. This is seen *inter alia* in provisions that set a maximum duration for lease contracts and in provisions that entitle the lessee to a wide extent to request prolongation of the agreement. The ambition to protect the lessee is clearest in Chapter 9 and 10. The provisions of Chapter 9 and 10 are completed with the provisions in the Act on the Lessee's Right to Preemtion (1985:658) according to which a lessee may preempt the sale of the land subject to a notice to the authorities for entry in the real estate register.

525. Chapter 12 regards the lease, not of land but of buildings or building areas or tenancy contracts (Sw. *hyra*). In general the provisions that apply to non-commercial tenancy contracts are mandatory in favour of the tenant. Chapter 12 sections 3–8 contain quite detailed provisions on the term of the contract and the forms for termination. Sections 9–18 regard impediments to the enjoyment of the tenancy. The provisions also give the tenant a substantial influence when it comes to repairs and modernization of buildings subject to tenancy contract. Sections 19–22 regard payment of the rent. The rent in non-commercial rental contracts is in principle required to correspond to the utility value rather than the market value as determined by the demand on the market. Rents are to a large extent negotiated collectively between organizations representing on the one hand land lords and on the other hand tenants subject to statutory provisions in the Act on Rent Negotiations (1978:304). Sections 23–27 regard the tenant's use of the rented apartment. In principle a duty of care is placed on the tenant, including a responsibility for people that have entered the apartment. Damage liability does in principle require proof of negligence. Sections 28–31 regard bailment, seizure and bankruptcy. Sections 32–40 regard transfer by the tenant of the rights under his contract and sub-leases. The general principle is that the tenant may not transfer the contract without the approval of the land lord. The general principle is however modified through a large number of exceptions. Sections 42–44 regard termination of the contract for breach (Sw: *förverkande av hyresrätten*). The provisions are detailed, but the general policy is that a tenant to a large extent shall have the right to regain the contract by curing the breach (Sw: *besittningsskydd*). Sections 45–55 are also quite detailed and regard the right for the tenant to require prolongation of the tenancy contract and provision entitling the parties to settle dispute about the level of the rent in prolongation cases under the auspices of a special court for lease and tenancy matters (Sw: *hyresnämnd*). Sections 56–60 regard commercial rental contracts. Under these provisions the tenant does not have an enforceable right to prolongation of the contract. If however the conditions for prolongation set by the land lord are deemed unreasonable by the special court for tenancy matters and the land lord refuses to accept the conditions set by the court, the land lord is liable to pay damages to the tenant for the harm caused by the termination. The final provisions in sections 61–73 regard special matters including provisions on the procedure in tenancy disputes.

Chapter 7. Compromise Settlement

526. Compromise settlement contracts are not considered to be a specific kind of contracts. Rather the settlement draws its nature from the underlying contract. Thus a settlement can appear as a pure release of the obligations of the other party (Sw: *eftergift*) or appear as a new agreement substituting an old agreement subject to a dispute. It is common to refer to such new agreements – based on a release conditional upon new undertakings – as a novation.[260]

527. Compromise settlement agreements concluded during court proceedings are frequently requested to be confirmed by a court judgment. Clear undertakings to perform under the settlement agreement are then immediately enforceable.

260. See no. 406 above.

Chapter 8. Suretyship

528. The statutory rules on suretyship (Sw. *borgen*) in the Commercial Code Chapter 10 sections 8–12 date back to 1734. The law on suretyship has since then to a large extent been developed by courts. The general contractual principles are the following.

529. A suretyship agreement is accessory to the main agreement. A suretyship agreement may be of two kinds, either amounting to an obligation to perform what the obligee cannot perform himself (Sw: *enkel borgen*) or an obligation to perform jointly and severally with the obligee (Sw: *proprieborgen*). The latter kind of suretyship is more common.

530. Upon performance the surety gets redress against the obligee. The creditor has a duty towards the surety to be active in order to maintain the right to redress, *inter alia* by maintaining his right to claim the obligee. A failure to maintain the redress leads to a reduction of the surety's obligations towards the creditor.

531. In cases where more than one surety has assumed obligations under a surety without stipulating a divided responsibility for the obligee, they are jointly and severally responsible toward the obligor.

Chapter 9. Pledge

532. The statutory rules on pledge of chattels (Sw. *pant*) in the Commercial Code Chapter 10 sections 1–7 also date back to 1734. Like the law on suretyship, the law on pledge has since then to a large extent been developed by courts. The general contractual principles are the following.

533. A pledge cannot only be made in respect of chattels, but also in respect of a right such as the right to shares, a right to payment or delivery or the right to yield or dividend.

534. The pledge is a security right characterized by the creditor's right to procure payment of a debtor's debt directly out of the pledged chattel or right without having to initiate seizure proceedings. A pledge can be constituted by operation of statutory law (e.g., pursuant to provisions in the Commission Agency Act) or pursuant to an agreement. The former is known as statutory pledge (Sw: *legal panträtt*) and the latter is known as conventional pledge (Sw: *konventionell panträtt).*

A pledge gives rise to two areas of legal relationships. There is one relationship between the pledgee and third parties (such as the pledgor's other creditors or his bankruptcy estate) that is of a property law nature. There is also one relationship between the pledgee and the pledgor that is of a contractual nature.

535. If the pledge is made in respect of chattels, it is debated whether the yield falling from the property is included in the pledge. The prevailing view is that the pledgee – unless otherwise agreed – has no right to the yield.[261]

536. The pledgee has an obligation of best effort to maintain the value of the pledged property. The pledgee is liable to damages should he by any negligent act cause physical damage to the value of the pledged chattel. In cased of pledges of rights, the pledgee is under a duty to see to it that the right is not lost due to statutory limitations. He is also under a duty to minimize the value loss that a pledged object inevitable may undergo (e.g., due to physical deterioration).[262]

537. The pledgee has the right to transfer his right to the pledged object. He can also pledge his right (Sw: *återpantsättning*). Usually, a transfer of the right to the pledge or a pledge of the pledge is made together with a transfer or pledge of the underlying claim for performance that the pledge is intended to secure. The right to transfer or pledge of the pledgee can be limited or excluded pursuant to the pledge agreement.[263]

538. If the pledgor does not perform, the pledgee may procure payment out of the pledged object. Unless otherwise is agreed the forms for payment procurement is regulated in Chapter 10 section 2 of the Commercial Code. In principle this means

261. See G. Lennander, Panthavarens skyldigheter, p. 114 (1977).
262. See *supra*, pp 63 et seq.
263. See *supra*, pp 153 et seq.

that the pledged object shall be valued by an independent person, whereupon the pledgor may elect to redeem the object (ie. pay the value) or let the pledgee sell the object at a public auction. He can also choose to let the pledgee keep the pledged object at the set value. Any balance shall be paid by the pledgor. The old statutory rules are regularly set aside by agreement to the effect that the pledgee may sell the pledged object without observing any formalities provided that he acts with due care and accounts for his activities. The pledgee may also elect to initiate seizure proceedings in lieu of a valuation as prescriped by the statutory provision.[264] An agreement that the pledgor's right to the pledged object shall be forfeited is invalid; see section 37 of the Contracts Act (the provision is also known as *lex commissoria*).[265]

264. See *supra* pp 239 et seq.
265. See *supra*, pp 252 et seq.

Chapter 10. Loans

539. The statutory rules on loans of chattels (Sw. *saklån*) in the Commercial Code Chapter 11 sections 1 and 3 dates back to 1734. Court cases are scarce and quite old. Contract for loans of chattels are treated in analogy with other beneficial agreements. This means that loan contracts become binding upon the transfer of the object of the loan.

540. The loaner has a duty of care subject to damage liability due to negligence. In general the burden of proof is reversed; in order to avoid damage liability the loaner has to prove that damage to the object of the loan was not due to negligence on his side. A loaner may not retain the object of the loan in order to claim payment or other performance by the other party unless the object has been pledged or the loaner has had necessary expenses in order to maintain the object of the loan.

Chapter 11. Contracts with the Government and Other Public Administrations

541. A contract between a public body, for instance a municipality, and a private actor is basically treated in the same way as a contract between two private actors, i.e., the general contract law and law of obligations apply. There is no special category in contract law for 'public contracts' or 'administrative contracts' and the former strongly emphasized divide between public law and private law is disappearing with increased privatization. However, this is not to say that a contract where one of the parties is a public authority might not involve certain problems which are not present in contract relations between private partners. For instance, a municipality which intends to acquire land for the purpose of placing a park on the spot in question, may in the contract negotiations with the owner of the land, threaten to expropriate the real estate in question if the price is not acceptable for the municipality. In other words, a public body has power and instruments in the contract negotiations not available for private actors. It is true, that such behaviour during the negotiations might render the contract void due to duress or unconscionability, but this might be difficult to prove for the private actor. At the interpretation of a contract it may also be of importance that one of the parties is a public body; the court might have to take into consideration rules in public law which might influence how the content of the contract should be understood (Madell, Tom, Avtal mellan kommuner och enskilda – Avtalsslut och rättsverkningar, 2000, p. 14).

542. Furthermore, a public authority may not arrange through contract such matters that are to be determined by the public body as an authority (Sw: '*myndighetsutövning*'). For instance, a public servant cannot through contract agree with a person applying for a driver's license, that the license will be issued; here the public body, in this case the state authority Transportstyrelsen has to take a decision to issue (or not issue) the license. The remedies differ between a (breach of) contract, on the one hand, and decision taken by the public body in its capacity as public authority. Remedies available for a breach of contract are of different kinds with the most important being damages, whereas the remedy against the public decision is appeal. As a general rule, decisions by public authority, i.e., administrative decisions, are handled in the administrative court system, whereas breach of contract, if taken to court, would be handled by the regular courts (Sw: '*allmänna domstolar*').

543. A public authority's freedom of contract is not always clear. For instance, it cannot through contract with a private person, limit the freedom that politically elected bodies have to take decisions. If, for instance, in the case with the real estate property transaction mentioned above, the politically elected representatives of the municipality were to determine, after the purchase of the land, that the land should not become a park but should instead be used for building family houses, the seller of the land cannot have the contract declared void or collect damages for unjust enrichment, even if he would have received a much better price, had it been clear already at the conclusion of the contract that the land was to be used for housing purposes.

544. A special form of contract between public actors and private actors is the contract which has come about as the result of a public procurement procedure. The EU Directives 2004/18/EG and 2004/17/EU are the basis for the extensive regulation found in the Swedish Public Procurement Act (2007:1091) and the Act on Public Procurement within the Area of Water, Energy, Transport and Postal Services (2007:1092). Here, special rules apply, for instance with regard to providing information, with regard to the formation of contract and with regard to the validity and remedies. The principles of non-discrimination, openness, mutual recognition and proportionality should be adhered to in the process for the overall purpose of promoting competition. A new EU Directive on Public Procurement has been adopted by the European Parliament (2014/24/EU) but has not yet (2014) been implemented in Sweden.

Chapter 12. Contract of Partnership

545. The law on partnership is set forth in the Act on Partnerships (Sw: *Lag 1980:1102 om handelsbolag och enkla bolag*). If two or more parties agree to commonly conduct a business activity and they have registered the business in the trade register (Sw: *handelsregister*), an unlimited trade partnership has been created (Sw: *handelsbolag*). The statutory provisions on unlimited trade partnerships are contained in Chapter 2 of the Act. An unlimited trade partnership is a separate legal person. The partners may each one of them represent the partnership. If a partner however exceeds his authority in dealings with a third person and the person realized or should have realized this, the partnership is not bound by the legal acts done by the partner.[266] The partners are jointly and severally liable for the obligations of the commercial partnership. An indefinite agreement for a commercial partnership may be terminated by a partner at any time. The partnership shall then be dissolved within six months. The partnership shall also be dissolved at once if a partner terminates the agreement due to substantial breach by another partner or there is important ground for termination (Sw: *viktig grund*). The same applies in case of a partner's death.

546. Another kind of trade partnership arises when one of the partners (Sw: *kommanditdelägare*) limits his liability for the obligations of the partnership and leaves unlimited responsibility on at least one of the other partners (Sw: *komplementärer*). Such a partnership constitutes a limited trade partnership. The statutory provisions on limited trade partnerships are contained in Chapter 3 of the Act. A partner with limited liability may not represent the partnership and the death of such a partner does not require dissolution of the partnership.

547. Agreements on unlimited and limited partnerships take on a corporate character and are mostly studied as a part of the law of associations.

548. Beside unlimited and limited partnerships there is a third kind of partnership, general partnership (Sw: *enkelt bolag*) that arise immediately upon the conclusion of a partnership agreement – characterized by the fact that the partners agree to actively cooperate for a common goal. Such a goal may be to conduct a business activity although the partnership is not registered or any other common goal. The statutory provisions on common partnerships are contained in Chapter 4 of the Act. Unlike trade partnerships, a common partnership is not a separate legal person. Only the partners that participate in common legal acts are (jointly and severally) liable. A corollary is that a common partnership cannot acquire rights or own property. Rights arising due to common legal acts pertain to the participating partners and property that shall be devoted or used for the common purpose belong to the partner in possession of the property.

266. Compare Ch. 1 above.

Chapter 13. Quasi-contracts

549. The concept of quasi-contract is not a legally defined concept in Swedish law and it seems to be used in different ways in different jurisdictions. In Sweden, the concept has been used for a long time (going back at least to the beginning of the nineteenth century, see Grönfors, Avtalsgrundande rättsfakta, 1993, p. 99) and it has been used by the courts as a means to move the borders of what is basically non-contractual relationships into what is called 'contract like' relationships, thereby creating contractually based liability for the party who is considered to have acted negligently and thereby caused the harm.[267]

550. The courts take the opportunity to construct quasi-contracts when they find that the parties are in a type of relationship which involves obligations of some sort between them. For instance, through the construction of quasi-contract, the courts have made parties who have caused harm by not taking action in a certain situation liable, where – if the relationship had been considered non-contractual – inactivity would not have given the injured person any legal right to compensation. Quasi contract is often considered to be at hand for shops, restaurants, etc. vis-à-vis people entering the premises, where the courts construct a contract-like obligation for the owner *vis-à-vis* visitors to protect them from harm.[268]

§1. Negotiorum Gestio

551. Under Swedish law *negotiorum gestio* means 'performing services without a mandate' (Sw: *tjänster utan uppdrag*). This happens when somebody, without having a mandate from or acting as agent for another person, voluntarily protects this person's interests by providing service to this person, for instance by taking care of his property to protect it from damage that would otherwise have occurred. Whether the owner in such a situation has a duty to reimburse the gestor for his expenses is not clear; there is no contractual relation between the owner and the gestor. Furthermore, if the gestor acts as an agent for the owner/principal in order to voluntarily take care of the interests of the principal, it is not clear if such an act is binding on the principal.[269]

§2. Enrichment without Cause

552. Another consequence of the construction of a quasi-contract is that it might provide a right to restitution in situations where such a right would otherwise be difficult to find under Swedish law.[270] The right to restitution in situations of unjust

267. *Supra*, nos 79 et seq.
268. Supreme Court cases NJA 1987 p. 692, NJA 2001 p. 878.
269. Adlercreutz & Gorton, II, 2011, p. 162.
270. See the Danish author Andersen, Mads Bryde, Grundlæggende aftaleret 2008, p. 230. The law is similar in Denmark and Sweden.

enrichment builds on the principle that an enrichment without a legal ground (Sw: *förmögenhetsförskjutning utan rättsgrund*) should be recovered. The law on unjust enrichment is not very developed in Swedish law, and there are opposing views among Swedish jurists whether it is recognized as a general principle of law. 'The legal category of restitution or unjustified enrichment has traditionally had a weak position in Swedish law, albeit given some credit in contractual relations, some quasi-contractual relations and in cases of payments made in error, *condictio indebiti*',[271] but, on the other hand, ' … unjust enrichment has now become an argument which occurs so often, in so many different settings, that one could plausibly argue that it has assumed the form of a legal principle'.[272] There exists no particular legislation regarding unjust enrichment but a general principle on mutual restitution of performances applies when, for instance, a contract is terminated due to invalidity. Some Supreme court cases from later decades, for instance NJA 1989 p. 268, NJA 1993 p. 13 and NJA 2007 p. 519 indicate that the principle is – at least to some extent – recognized in Swedish law.

553. According to a modern textbook the following requirements should be fulfilled for restitution due to unjust enrichment under Swedish law.[273]

§3. Money Paid but Not Due (*Condictio indebiti*)

554. If somebody pays money to a person by mistake, i.e., where the person who receives the payment does not have any legal claim or right to the money, for instance when an employer by mistake pays to high a salary to an employee, the main rule is that the payment shall be restituted. This is called *condictio indebiti*, a principle which has its roots in Roman law. No particular legislation about *condictio indebiti* exists in Sweden, but various exceptions to the principle have been established through case law. If the person who has received the payment was in good faith when he received the money and thereafter has either used the money or established himself according to the economic circumstances, the person who made the payment by mistake may not have a right to get the money back.

271. Quote from J. Munukka, Civil Law Consequences of Corruption in Sweden, Stockholm Centre for Commercial Law Årsbok II, 2010, p. 299.

272. *Supra*, p. 305. See for an argumentation about unjust enrichment as an increasingly recognized principle, M. Schultz, Nya argumentationslinjer i förmögenhetsrätten – Obehörig vinst rediviva, SvJt 2009, pp 946 et seq., particularly p. 952, and Obehörig vinst-motiveringar, SvJt 2012, pp 372 et seq.

273. Ramberg-Ramberg, Allmän avtalsrätt, 2014, p. 244 building on Schultz, SvJt 2009, p. 956): (1) There should be 'enrichment', (2) The enrichment should be unjustified, i.e., without cause (Sw: *obehörig*), (3) The enrichment should have taken place at the expense of another, (4) There should not be any legally recognized excuse for the enrichment.

Selected Bibliography

BOOKS

Adlercreutz, A. *Högsta domsmakten i Sverige under 200 år. Del 2 Högsta domstolen och civilrätten.* (Nerenius och Santérus Stockholm 1989).
Adlercreutz, A. & L. Gorton. *Avtalsrätt I.* (13 ed., Juristförlaget 2011).
Adlercreutz, A. & L. Gorton. *Avtalsrätt II.* (6 ed., Juristförlaget 2010).
Andersen, M.B. *Grundlæggende aftaleret.* (3 ed., Gjellerup 2008).
Arvidsson, N. & P. Samuelsson. *Om avtals uppkomst: Vänbok till Axel Adlercrutz* (Juristförlaget 2007).
Beale, H.G. et al. *Contract – Cases & Materials.* (5 ed., Oxford University Press 2008).
Bengtsson, B. *Särskilda avtalstyper I.* (Norstedt 1971).
Bernitz, U. *Standardavtalsrätt.* (8 ed., Norstedts juridik 2013). Bernitz, U. *Finna rätt: Juristens källmaterial och arbetsmetoder.* (11 ed., Norstedts Juridik 2011).
Bernitz, U. *Svensk och europeisk marknadsrätt.* 2. ed., Norstedts Juridik 2009).
Cartwright, J. *Contract Law – An Introduction to the English Law of Contract for the Civil Lawyer.* (Hart Publishing 2007).
Giertsen, J. *Avtaler.* (Universitetsforlaget 2014).
Gerhard, P. & H. Norinder. *Marknadsrättens grunder.* (2. ed., Gleerups 2011).
Gorton, L. *The Nordic Tradition: Application of Boilerplate Clauses under Swedish Law.* p. 276, in Cordero-Moss, G. [ed.], Boilerplate Clauses, International Commercial Contracts and the Applicable Law – Common Law Contract Models and Commercial Transactions Subject to Civilian Governing Laws (Cambridge University Press 2011).
Grönfors, K. *Avtalsgrundande rättsfakta.* (Nerenius och Santérus 1993).
Grönfors, K. *Ställningsfullmakt och bulvanskap.* (Norstedt 1964).
Göransson, U. *Kolliderande standardavtal.* (Iustus 1988).
Hellner, J., Hager, R., & A. Persson. *Speciell avtalsrätt II.* (5 ed., Norstedts Juridik 2010).
Hellner, J. *Rättsteori.* (Juristförlaget 1994).
Hellner, J. & M. Radetzki. *Skadeståndsrätt.* (8 ed., Norstedts Juridik 2010).
Hessler, H. *Allmän sakrätt.* (Institutet för rättsvetenskaplig forskning Stockholm 1973).
Ingvarsson, T. *Ogiltighet och rättsföljd.* (Norstedts Juridik 2012).
Johansson, S. *Svensk associationsrätt i huvuddrag.* (10. ed., Norstedts 2011).
Lennander, G. *Panthavarens skyldigheter vid pantavtal om lös egendom.* (Almqvist & Wiksell International 1977).
Lindskog, S. *Skiljeförfarande: en kommentar.* (Norstedts 2005).

Madell, T-E. *Avtal mellan kommuner och enskilda – Avtalsslut och rättsverkningar.* (Norstedts Juridik 2000).
Madell, T-E. *Det allmänna som avtalspart.* (Norstedts Juridik 1998).
Mellqvist, M. & I. Persson. *Fordran och skuld.* (8 ed., Iustus Uppsala 2007).
Millqvist, G. *Financial Leasing: om det finansiella leasingavtalets civilrättsliga innebörd och reglering.* (Juridiska föreningen i Lund 1986).
Munukka, J. *Civil Law Consequences of Corruption.* in Sweden Stockholm Centre for Commercial Law Årsbok II, (Visby 2010).
Murray, C. et al. *Schmitthoff: The Law and Practice of International Trade.* (Sweet & Maxwell 2012).
Nordell, P.J. *Marknadsrätten – en introduktion.* (5 ed., Norstedts Juridik 2010).
Ramberg, C. & J. Ramberg. *Allmän avtalsrätt.* (Norstedts Juridik 2014).
Ramberg, J. & J. Herre. *Allmän köprätt: Det köprättsliga regelsystemet och marknadspraxis.* (3 ed., Norstedts Juridik 2009).
Rodhe, K. *Obligationsrätt* (Norstedt 1984).
Rodhe, K. *Handbok i sakrätt* (Norstedt 1985).
Sefton-Green, R. [ed.]. *Mistake, Fraud and Duties to Inform in European Contract Law.* (Cambridge University Press 2005).
Simonsen, L. *Prekontraktuellt ansvar: det alminnelige prekontraktuelle ansvar, ansvar ved gjennomföring av anbudskonkurranser.* (Universitetsforlaget 1997).
Svensson, O. *Avtalsfrihet och rättvisa: en rättsfilosofisk studie.* (Juristförlaget Lund Visby 2012).
Tiberg, H. & D. Lennhammer. *Skuldebrev, växel och check.* (7 ed., Fritze 1995).
Ussing, H. Aftaler paa formuerettens omraade. (3 ed., Gads forlaget 1950).
Wilhelmsson, T. Standardavtal och oskäliga avtalsvillkor. (3 ed., Talentum 2008).
Zachariasson, L. *Direktkrav: Om rätt att rikta anspråk mot gäldenärens gäldenär.* (Iustus Uppsala 1999).

Articles

Herre, J. *Svensk rättspraxis: Förmögenhetsrätt 1978-2004.* SvJT, p. 549-800 (2005).
Ingvarsson, T. *Spel och osedliga avtal.* SvJT, p. 751 (2004).
Kleineman, J. *Allmänna principer för ogiltighetspåföljdens inträdande.* JT, p. 808 (1997/98).
Kleineman, J. *De offentliga rättssubjektens avtalskompetens.* JT, p. 958 (1994/95).
Ramberg, J. *Medveten otydlighet som avtalsrättsligt problem.* JT, p. 358 (1992/93).
Schultz, M. *Nya argumentationslinjer i förmögenhetsrätten: Obehörig vinst rediviva.* SvJT, p. 946 (2009).
Schultz, M. *Obehörig vinst-motiveringar.* SvJT, p. 372 (2012).

Electronic sources

Guiding Principles of European Contract Law, *Société de legislation (2008),*http://www.legiscompare.fr/Site-web/IMG/pdf/19_Guiding Principles.pdf, p. 81 (accessed 28 Oct. 2013).

Index

The numbers here refer to paragraph numbers.

Acceptance, agreement and reciprocity
  CISG Article 18(3), 136
  delay in transmission of, 143–144
  effective, 137
  inactivity, 138
  late, 141–142
  modification, 146–147
  offer (*see* Offer and acceptance)
  performance of action, 137
  time of, 139–140
  withdrawal of, 145
  written confirmation
analogous application, 152
commercial contracts, 151
evidentiary value, 149
message, 148
order, 152
with or without passivity, 150, 154
Accessory contracts, 69
Administrative contracts, 541–544
Agency
  brokers (*see* Brokers)
  commission (*see* Commission agency)
  under Contract Act
acting outside authority, 480–483
differences, authority and mandate, 473–474
establishment/mandate, 465–469
passive authority, 478–479
position, 470–472
principal's tolerance, 477
ratification, 477
termination, 475–476
  distributors, 496–497
  regulation
agent action, 460, 463
commission agent, 463
intermediaries, 464
meaning, agent, 463
private company, 463
  self-employed commercial agents, 488–492
Agreement and quid pro quo (reciprocity)
  common law doctrine of consideration, 179
  gratuitous promises, 180
  intention to create legal relations
acceptance period, 177
burden of proof, 178
English law, 174
judicial act, 175, 176
  offer (*see* Offer and acceptance)
  specific matter/particular form, 160
  standard terms, 167–170
Agricultural lease, 524–525
Aleatory contracts, 65, 503
Anglo-American parol evidence rule, 190
Arbitration clauses, 300

Bailment
  bailor protection, 499
  bankrupt, 502
  contract and liability rules, 501
  exercise good care, another person property, 498, 500
  meaning, 498
  parties' obligations, 499
  real contract, 498
  transaction, 498
Bankruptcy, 240
Battle of forms, 172–173
Belgian Breyne Act of 1971, 520
Bilateral and unilateral contracts, 62
Brokers
  commission, 495
  economic interest, 494
  independent intermediary/middleman/agent, 493
  rule, 493

standards, 494
types, 494
Building contracts
construction/repair/real estate, 520
consumer protection, 520
regulation, 520
standard form (AB 04), 521–522
Burden of proof
general observations, 192–193
obligation of means and outcomes, 194–195

Capacity of parties, valid contract
bankruptcy, 240
insanity/mental disturbances, 237–238
married women, 239
minors, 233–236
moral person, 241
Civil and commercial law, 34
Commercial lease, 524–525
Commission agency
banks, 485
Commission Agency Act (2009), 463
contract expires/termination, 486
damages, 487
principal function, 484
regulation, 463
relationship, 485
sales/purchase contract, 484
third party performance, 484
Commission Agency Act, 117, 122, 138, 220, 375, 403, 425, 463, 485, 518, 534
Commutative and aleatory contracts, 65
Compromise settlement, 526–527
Consensual contracts, 59
Convention on the International Sale of Goods (1980), 504–506

Damages
actual, 299
breach of precontractual duty, 209
compensation, 209
and exemption clauses
agreed payment for non-performance, 451–454
assessment, currency, 450
'casus mixtus cum culpa' principle, 418
contractual and non-contractual, 419
full compensation, 429–432
harm (*see* Harm and damages)
liability, negligence (*see* Liability for negligence)
monetary redress, 449
non-payment, interest, 443–448
rights, 418
Defects in consent
dishonesty, 262–266
doctrine of failed assumptions, 243–245
duress, coercion and undue influence (section 28 and 29), 246–250
fraud (section 30), 251
gross disparity, 274–275
misrepresentation, 267–273
mistake (section 32), 254–261
usury (section 31), 252–253
void contract, 242
Definition of contract
binding character, 41–42
declaration of will, 35
freedom of contract, 37–40
mandatory rules, 43–48
rights 'in personam' and rights 'in rem', 49
will, intent and reliance, 36
Discharge by agreement, 404–405
Dishonesty (Contact Act section 33)
general clause, 264
invalidity rule, 262
party's intention, 265
seldom, 266
subsequent circumstances, 263
Duress
performs, legal act, 248
pressure physical violence, 246
voidable contract, 247
Duty of loyalty, 96–103

Evidential requirement/proof
notary function, 191
parol evidence rule, 190
Formal requirements
CISG Article 11, 181
collective bargaining agreements, 184
consumer contract, 183
contracts under seal, 188
documentation, obligations of parties, 185
modifications, 187
oral agreements, 181
prerequisite for binding contract, 123
sale of real estate, 182
'solemn' contracts, 189
statutory duty, 186
written form, 123, 182–184

Formation of contract
  agreement and quid pro quo (reciprocity), 124–173
  burden of proof, 192–195
  conduct of the parties, 121
  evidential requirement/proof, 190–191
  formal requirements, 181–189
  liability and negotiations, 196–210
  negative contracting, 122
  passivity, 122
Frame contracts, 70
Freedom of contract
  consumer contract conditions, 40
  meaning, 37
  modification/setting aside, unreasonable terms, 39
  non-mandatory rules, 40
  parties, 38

Geography
  area, 2
  population, 3
  Scandinavian peninsula, Northern Europe, 1
  size, 1
Good faith and fair dealing
  cooperation, 104
  duty of loyalty, 96–103
  inconsistent behaviour, 105–111
Government contracts, 541–544
Gratuitous contracts, 63–64
Gross disparity, 274–275

Harm and damages
  act/omission, aggrieved party, 440
  certainty, 433–435
  foreseeability, 436–438
  mitigation, 441–442
  replacement transaction, proof of, 439

Inconsistent behaviour, 105–111
Initial impossibility, 277
Insanity/mental disorder persons, contract, 237–238
Intention
  agreement (*see* Agreement and quid pro quo (reciprocity))
  negotiations, 208
  parties, 265, 303–305, 308
Interpretation of contract
  awareness, 307
  clarity of wording, 309, 310
  contra proferentem rule, 320–321
  direct relevance, 314
  gap-filling activity, courts, 302
  indirect relevance, 313
  omitted term, 322–323
  parties intention, 303–305, 308
  preliminary negotiations, 312
  prima facie, 301
  references
contract/statement as whole, 316–317
enclosures, 308
standard agreement, specification and
  documents, 308
  rules, 302
  statements, 306
  term, 301
  terms to be given effect, 318–319
  verification/falsification, 311
  warranty, 315
  written contract, 308
Intuitu personae contracts, 66
Invalidity, contracts
  civil law and common law, 220
  clause on modification/setting aside, 228–232
  consequences, 218, 219
  Contracts Act, section 36, 217
  defects of will, 218
  degree of formality, 227
  duress/forgery, 214
  formal requirements, 226
  general principles, 211
  impossibility principle, 225
  legal capacity, parties, 213
  legal consequences, 287–292
  nullity, 212
  public policy/morality, 215
  restitution of performance, 216, 219
  statutory provisions, 220
  terms not agreed, 224
  total/partial, 211
  voidness and voidability, 221–223

Judiciary
  administrative court system, 31
  general court system, 29
  local and Supreme Court, 30
  specialized courts and jurisdiction, 32
  Supreme Court judges, 30

Index

Late acceptance, 141–142
Law of contracts
arbitration clauses, 300
classification
bilateral and unilateral, 62
commutative and aleatory, 65
consensual, 59
frame, 70
intuitu personae, 66
main and accessory, 69
nominate and innominate, 67
onerous and gratuitous, 63–64
real, 61
Solemn, 60
standard form, 68
definition (*see* Definition of contract)
development, Swedish Contract Law, 54–58
formal and evidential requirements, 191–195
formation (*see* Formation of contract)
influence of Roman Law, 50–53
interpretation (*see* Interpretation of contract)
liability and negotiations (*see* Liability and negotiations of contract)
penalty clauses, 296–299
privity (*see* Privity of Contract)
property (*see* Law of property and contract)
quasi-contracts (*see* Quasi-contracts)
remedies (*see* Remedies)
substantive validity (*see* Substantive validity conditions)
termination (*see* Termination of contract)
terms
express, 293
implied, 294
standard and exemption clauses, 295
torts (*see* Torts)
trust (*see* Trust)
Law of property and contract
conveyancing
agreement, 91
derivative and extinctive acquisition, 90
originate acquisition, 90
registration, 92–93
co-ownership, 86
drafting, 112
good faith (*see* Good faith and fair dealing)
legal and equitable ownership, 87
loan, 86
ownership, 84
'right in personam' and 'right in rem', 81, 82
rights, 83
sources (*see* Sources of Law of Contracts)
third parties, 83
transfer of property, 85
usufruct, 88–89
Lease
agricultural, 525
commercial, 524, 525
general provisions, 524
Land Code, 523
rights and obligations, 523
Legal consequences of invalidity
damages, 292
ex tunc, 287
nullity of contract, 288
performance of parties, 287
restitution, 289–291
Letters of intent, 162–164
Liability and negotiations of contract
Culpa in contrahendo, 204–205
damages, 209, 210
delictual/tortious, 200
doctrine of failed assumptions, 196
doctrine of precontractual, 200, 201
duty to inform
disclosure, 206
false representation, 207
fraud/usury, 196
general principle of loyalty, 200, 201
good faith, 202, 203
intention, 208
null and void, 196
party's conduct, 199
precontractual, 197–198
Sale of Goods Act, 196
Liability for negligence
agency, 425
breach of contract, 418, 420
defective performance, 426
direct and indirect losses, 424
force majeure, 427
guarantees, 421
non-performance amounts, 423
protection, parties, 428
third party performance, 420
wrongful termination/rescission, agreement, 422

Limitation of actions, 455–458
Loans, 539–540

Main and accessory contracts, 69
Minors, valid contract, 233–236
Misrepresentation
  banking and investment, 272
  failed assumptions, 273
  false statement, contract negotiations, 267
  full and accurate information, insurance contract, 268
  guarantee, 267
  marketing, 269
  Norwegian case, 272
  parties making, 273
  real estate, 271
  regulations, 268
  Sale of Goods Act, 269
  voidable, 267
Mistake
  declaration of intent, 254–259
  persons, 260
  substance, 261

Nominate and innominate contracts, 67
Non-performance of contract
  definition, 396
  interference, 397
  remedies, 396, 422, 423
Nordic legal family, 27
Notices
  Contracts Act, section 39, 159
  intent, requests and claims, 155
  knowledge, 159
  process, 156
  receiver, 159
  risk, 157, 158
  termination and rejection, 157
  withdrawal, 156
Novation, 406–408
Nullity of contract, 288

Offer and acceptance
  battle of forms, 172–173
  clauses on modification and merger, 165–166
  conflicts, standard and non-standard terms, 171
  creation, legal and natural persons, 128
  degree of definiteness, 161
  effective, 125, 126
  form of statement, 127
  identifiable recipients, 129
  intent, 124
  issued by offeror/offeree, 129
  legal act, 124
  letters of intent, 162–164
  notices, 155–159
  offreror, 126
  overreaching policy expression, 125
  precision, 130
  receiver, 131
  recognition, 125
  rejection, 135
  revocation, 133–134
  specific matter/particular form, 160
  standard terms, 167–170
  withdrawal, 132
Onerous and gratuitous contracts, 63–64

Partnership
  agreement, 547, 548
  liability, 545
  parties, 545
  trade, 545, 546
  unlimited and limited, 547–548
Payment
  business place and day, 388
  currency, 389–390
  invoice, 388
  transfer of funds, 388
Penalty clauses
  actual damages, 299
  compensation, 297
  delays, 297
  exemption, 297
  liquidated damages, 296, 297
  reasonability test, Contact Act section 36, 298
Performance of contract
  application for public permission, 395
  computation of time setting up by parties, 381
  cost, 391
  earlier, 385
  imputation of obligations, 392–394
  indefinite period, 375–376
  non-performance (*see* Non-performance)
  order of, 384
  partial, 382–383
  payment (*see* Payment)
  place of, 386–387
  price determination, 373–374

quality of, 372
time of, 377–380
Pledge of chattels
obligation, pledgee, 536
payment procurement, 538
rights, 533, 534
statutory rules, 532
transfer of rights, 537
yield, 535
Political history
beginning of 19th century, 8
Christian and Muslim faith, 6
establishment, universal suffrage, 10
Grand Epoch, 17th century, 7
independent and unified state, middle ages, 5
modern industrial state, end of 19th century, 9
monarchy constitutional, 7
parliamentary system, 18th centuries, 7
Political system, 11–12
Precontractual liability, 197–198
Primacy of legislation, 28
Prima facie interpretation, 308–311
Privity of contract
subcontracting (*see* Subcontract)
third parties (*see* Third parties, privity of contract)
transfer
obligations, 360–361
rights (*see* Transfer of contractual rights)
whole contractual position, 362
Public and private law, 33
Public policy, 278–279

Quasi-contracts
construction of, 80, 550
'contract like' relationships, 79
enrichment without cause, 552–553
liability, 549
negotiorum gestio, 551
non-contractual relationships, 549
parties, 80
payment *(condictio indebiti),* 554

Real contracts, 61
Real Estate Broker Act (2011), 519
Re-integra rule, section 39 of Contracts Act, 286
Rejection of offer, 135
Remedies
damages (*see* Damages)
defence of non-performance, 415–417
general principle and policy, 409–410
limitation of actions, 455–458
specific performance, 411–413
termination, 414
Revocation of offer, 133–134

Sale of goods
adoptions, 504
auction sales, 507
Convention on the International Sale of Goods, 504, 505
liability, seller's statements, 507
mandatory rights, consumers, 508
non-mandatory provisions, 504
party's liability, direct and indirect losses, 506
Sale of Goods Act (1990), 504
Self-employed commercial agents, 488–492
Service contracts
Consumer Services Act, 515
general rules, 513
good faith and fair dealing, 512
hire of work and skill, 509
legislation, 519
material and immaterial/intellectual services, 511
mixed, 510
obligations, 512
price, 516
regulation, 514, 519
relationship, 514
remedies, breach of contract, 517
types, 509, 518
Solemn contracts, 60
Sources of Law of Contracts
common law - precedents, 113
constitutional and ordinary acts, 113
hierarchy norm, 116–117
mercantile usages and customs, 113
ordinances, 113
practices and custom, 118–119
soft law instruments, 115
Supreme Court decisions, 114
Standard form contracts, 68
Standard terms, contract
adjust/set aside unreasonable terms, 170
agreed documents, 167
commercial transactions, 168
conditions, 167
consumer contracts, 169
and non-standard terms, 171

Strict liability, 421, 423, 427
Subcontract
  cause loss/damage to the creditor, 363
  debtor and the third party, 363, 364
  liability of main contractor, 365–366
  performance, 363, 364
  relationship with employer, 367–369
Substantive validity conditions
  defects in consent, 242–275
  existing and lawful cause, 276
  initial impossibility, 277
  invalidity (*see* Invalidity, contracts)
  mandatory regulation, 281–285
  morality, 280–281
  parties capacity, 233–241
  public policy, 278–279
  re-integra rule, 286
Suretyship
  agreement, 529
  creditor, 530
  obligations, 529–531
  responsibility, 531
  statutory rules, 528
Swedish economy
  developments, 13, 18
  export and import, 14
  foreign ownership of companies, 17
  industries, 14, 16
  small open economy, 13
  structural changes, 15
Swedish legal culture and system
  civil law tradition, 19
  Constitution, 21–22
  court system, 26
  international conventions/treaties, 23
  legislative cooperation, Nordic countries, 20
  sources of law, 24–25
  structure, 19

Termination of contract
  discharge by agreement, 404–405
  impossibility, frustration and hardship, 398
doctrine of failed assumptions, 398
modification and cease of obligations, 399–403
obligations, 398
term, 398
  non-performance (*see* Non-performance of contract)
  novation, 406–408
  performance (*see* Performance of contract)
Third parties, privity of contract, 324–334
  advantages
bilateral contract, 335
conditions of validity, 340
direct actions, 345–346
insurance, 337, 338
mandatory rules, 338
protection, 339
rights, 336, 339, 341
stipulator and promisor rights and duties, 342–344
  commission agency, 325
  construction projects, 330
  contractual relationship, 325
  exceptions, 331
  financial lease, 330
  liabilities, 329, 330, 333
  Maritime Code, 331
  meaning, 325
  obligation, 327
  oblique, paulian and direct actions, 370–371
  public contracts, 326
  regulation, 329
  rights of, 324
  subcontract, 363, 364
  subjective limitation, 328
  sue on other parties, 332
  transfer of property, 334
  transfer of rights, 347, 358–359
  transport of goods, 330, 331
Time of acceptance, 139–140
Torts
  and contractual liability, 73
  injured person choose action in tort/contract, 76
  and insurance, 71
  negligence, damage liability, 74
  pure economic loss, 75
  right to compensation, 77–78
  strict liability, 71
  term, 71
  tortfeasor, 71
  Tort Liability Act, 72
Transfer of contractual rights
  assignment, financial claim, 350
  bonds and stocks, 353
  effects of assignment, 356–357
  general law of obligations, 348
  negotiable documents of title, 355

negotiable instrument act, 351
performance and non-monetary performance, 349
promissory note, 351–353
against third parties, 358–359
third person, 347
Trust, 94–95

Usury/unfair exploitation, 252–253

Warranty, 315
Withdrawal
acceptance, 145
notices, 156
offer, 132